More Praise for *The I[*

Marc Abrahams is the editor and cofounder of the science humor magazine *Annals of Improbable Research* (*AIR*); its online counterpart, www.improbable.com; and the monthly e-newsletter *mini-AIR*. The founding father and master of ceremonies of the annual Ig Nobel Prize Ceremony at Harvard University, and a weekly columnist for *The Guardian* newspaper, Abrahams has a degree in applied mathematics from Harvard. He lives in Cambridge, Massachusetts.

The Ig Nobel Prizes

REWARDING THE WORLD'S UNLIKELIEST RESEARCH

Marc Abrahams

℗

A PLUME BOOK

PLUME
Published by the Penguin Group
Penguin Group (USA) Inc., 375 Hudson Street, New York, New York 10014, U.S.A.
Penguin Books Ltd, 80 Strand, London WC2R 0RL, England
Penguin Books Australia Ltd, 250 Camberwell Road, Camberwell, Victoria 3124, Australia
Penguin Books Canada Ltd, 10 Alcorn Avenue, Toronto, Ontario, Canada M4V 3B2
Penguin Books India (P) Ltd, 11 Community Centre, Panchsheel Park, New Delhi–110 017, India
Penguin Books (NZ), cnr Airborne and Rosedale Roads, Albany, Auckland 1310, New Zealand
Penguin Books (South Africa) (Pty) Ltd, 24 Sturdee Avenue, Rosebank,
Johannesburg 2196, South Africa

Penguin Books Ltd, Registered Offices: 80 Strand, London WC2R 0RL, England

Published by Plume, a member of Penguin Group (USA) Inc.
Previously published in a Dutton edition.

First Plume Printing, September 2004
10   9   8   7   6   5   4   3   2   1

Copyright © Marc Abrahams, 2002
All rights reserved

The author and publisher are grateful to the following for permission to publish copyrighted material:

Chemistry & Industry for their editorial "We Are Amused" © *Chemistry & Industry*, 1996.
BMJ Publishing Group for the use of images from *BMJ* vol. 319, 1999, pp. 1596–1600.

 REGISTERED TRADEMARK–MARCA REGISTRADA

The Library of Congress has cataloged the Dutton edition as follows:

Abrahams, Marc
    The Ig Nobel prizes / by Marc Abrahams
        p. cm.
    ISBN 0-525-94753-1 (hc.)
    ISBN 0-452-28573-9 (pbk.)
    1. Science–Miscellanea. 2. Research–Miscellanea. I. Title.
Q173 .A18 2003
502'.07–dc21   2003049081

Printed in the United States of America
Original hardcover design by Leonard Telesca

CONTENTS

The
Ig Nobel
Prizes

INTRODUCTION

 This book exists because it's difficult to believe that these people really did these things. So, here is the evidence. Here are detailed accounts of a good many of the Ig Nobel Prize winners, and what they did, and the reasons (or, if you prefer, the "reasons") why they did what they did.

These triumphs of persistence over improbability beg for some sort of short, bracing introduction. Therefore, here is an introductory chapter in which you will find:

- What's an Ig?
- How It Began, Briefly
- How the Winners Are Chosen
- The Ceremony
- Controversy
- How to Read This Book

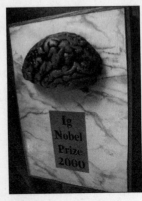

The Ig Nobel Prize that was awarded in 2000

WHAT'S AN IG?

Some people covet it, others flee from it. Some see it as a hallmark of civilization, others as a scuff mark. Some laugh with it, others laugh at it. Many praise it, a few condemn it, others are just mystified. And many people are madly in love with it.

It is the Ig Nobel Prize.

Everything that has won an Ig Nobel Prize shares this quality: it first makes people LAUGH, then makes them THINK. *What* people think is up to them.

The winners are a varied lot. Doesn't matter if what they've done is naughty or nice, important or inconsequential, intelligent or idiotic, famous or forgotten. If they have done something that first makes people LAUGH, then makes them THINK, that's all it takes.

The winners and their achievements are akin to what Sherlock Holmes craved in his famous collection of newspaper clippings:

"He took down the great book in which, day by day, he filed the agony columns of the various London journals. 'Dear me!' said he, turning over the pages, 'what a chorus of groans, cries, and bleatings! What a rag-bag of singular happenings! But surely the most valuable hunting-ground that ever was given to a student of the unusual!'"

But Sherlock Holmes was of course fictional. The Ig Nobel Prize winners are real.

Each year, ten Ig Nobel Prizes are awarded to people whose achievements "cannot or should not be reproduced." The "Igs" (as they are known) honor people who have done remarkably goofy things—some admirable, some perhaps otherwise.

These things can be difficult to believe. That is why the Ig Nobel Board of Governors publishes information that you can use to verify and savor the details.

That is also why the winners are invited to come to the Ig Nobel Prize Ceremony, which is held each October at Harvard University. The winners must travel at their own expense, and for many it is apparently worth the cost. A friendly, standing-room-only audience of 1,200 welcomes them with warm wild applause, and paper airplanes.

In a unique ritual, genuine Nobel Laureates physically hand the Ig Nobel Prizes to the new Ig Nobel Prize winners. Each time this occurs, it is a magical instant—at that moment it feels as if the universe has two opposite ends, and these two opposite ends have somehow managed to meet and touch. Nobel Laureate and Ig Nobel Laureate look each other in the eye, each filled with gleeful wonder.

How It Began, Briefly

The Ig Nobel Prize Ceremony was born not long after I unexpectedly became the editor of a magazine called *The Journal of Irreproducible Results*. *The Journal* was started in 1955 by Alex Kohn and Harry Lipkin, two eminent and very funny scientists in Israel, but it eventually fell into other hands and withered to near-extinction. In 1990, I mailed off some articles to see whether this journal (which I had never seen) still existed, and if so whether it might print them. Several weeks later came a telephone message from a man who said he was the publisher, that he'd gotten the articles, and would I be the magazine's editor.

As the editor of a science magazine, even a funny one, I was besieged by people who wanted my help in winning a Nobel Prize. I always explained that I had no influence on these matters, but they invariably told me in great detail what they'd done and why they deserved a prize. In some cases, they were right. They deserved a prize, but not a Nobel Prize.

And so, together with everyone I could talk into helping out, I started the Ig Nobel Prize Ceremony. Alex Kohn suggested naming it after the "Ignoble Prize," a fictional award he and Harry Lipkin had described years before.

We held the first Ig Nobel Prize Ceremony in October 1991.

The publishers of that magazine, by the way, had a corporate shuffle, and made it clear that a science humor magazine was no longer for them. Rather than watch it go down the tubes, we all left and immediately started a new magazine, the *Annals of Improbable Research* (*AIR*). I have fond memories of the day when four Nobel Laureates each separately informed me, with appropriate cackles, that I am an *AIR*head. *AIR* is the proud home base of the Ig.

It cannot be overstated that the Ig Nobel Prize winners and their accomplishments are real.

At the conclusion of one Ig Nobel Prize Ceremony, a female journalist from England climbed onto the stage and accosted a Nobel Laureate, who had just helped hand out the awards.

"This was your first Ig, wasn't it?" she asked the distinguished scientist. "Did you enjoy it?" "Oh, yes," he said, eyes crinkling in delight. "Those people were so funny! Can you imagine if they'd really done those things?"

The reporter gave a low chuckle. "They *did* do those things."

The Nobel Laureate was silent for a moment. Then he, too, gave a low chuckle. And almost every year since, he has returned to the ceremony to shake hands with each new crop of Ig Nobel Prize winners.

HOW THE WINNERS ARE CHOSEN

Who chooses the winners? The Ig Nobel Board of Governors. Who are the Ig Nobel Board of Governors? Ah. The group comprises the editors of the *Annals of Improbable Research* (the science humor magazine I edit), and a considerable number of scientists (including, yes, several Nobel Laureates), journalists, and others in a variety of fields in a variety of countries. The group never meets at a single gathering. We keep no records of who sent in nominations or, for that matter, of who exactly is on the committee. There is a tradition that for the final decision, we grab some passerby from the street, to add a little balance.

Where do the nominations come from? Anywhere. Everywhere. Anyone can nominate anyone for an Ig Nobel Prize, and pretty much anyone does. We receive several thousand nominations each year, among them quite a few persons nominating themselves (to date, only one Prize has ever been awarded to a self-nominee—the Norwegian team of Barheim and Sandvik, who researched the effects of ale, garlic, and sour cream on the appetite of leeches).

Generally, those who are selected can turn down the Prize if they truly believe it might cause them professional difficulties with bosses, governments, or the like. But in the twelve years that Prizes have been given, only a small handful have declined. In recent years, most winners have chosen to attend the ceremony or, when finances or other circumstances made that difficult, at least send an acceptance speech.

The winners who come to collect their Prizes always receive a warm welcome. If someone is sporting enough to come celebrate their goofy achievement in public, the audience and the organizers always give them an appreciative, if chuckling, tip of the cap.

THE CEREMONY

If you win an Ig Nobel Prize, the best part is that you get to star in the Ig Nobel Prize Ceremony, and be the upside-down-buttered toast of the town.

The ceremony began as something giddy in the dead of night, with 350 people crammed inside a museum at the Massachusetts Institute of Technology. That first year, 1991, we invited four Nobel Laureates to come help hand out the Prizes. All four showed up, wearing Groucho glasses, sashes, fezzes, and other stylishly sportive attire. The public was invited to attend, and almost instantly snapped up all the tickets. Reporters came, too, and on that evening everyone had the gleeful feeling of sneaking something really different into being. The emphasis here is on the word "sneak," because we all felt as though sooner or later some authority figure would rush in and tell us to stop this nonsense and go home. But no one did, and it was a wild success, and the next year we had to move it to the largest meeting place at MIT.

Thereafter, nominations came in a never-ending flood, and every year, spectators, winners, and Nobel Laureates came from great distances to take part in the ceremony.

After the Fourth First Annual Ig Nobel Prize Ceremony in 1994, a dyspeptic MIT administrator tried to ban the event. Puzzled but almost amused, the Ig Nobel Board of Governors simply moved everything two miles up the road, where it now has a permanent home at Sanders Theatre, Harvard University's oldest, largest, and most stately meeting place. Several Harvard student groups cosponsor the event together with the *Annals of Improbable Research.* Many Harvard and MIT faculty members, students, and administrators, and many other people as well, are part of what is now a year-round, all-volunteer organizing effort.

The ceremony itself has grown ever more complex, a jaunty meld of every dignified convention with its every off-balance antidote, heaped high with essence of Academy Awards, coronation, circus, football game, opera, booby hatch, laboratory accident, and the old Broadway show *Hellzapoppin.* Each year more goodies are jammed around, between, and atop the awarding of the ten new Ig Nobel Prizes. My role as master of ceremonies has been likened to that of Kermit the Frog, trying desperately to keep some thread of calm and dignity in a theater filled with scintillant lunatics, each swinging full tilt through his or her own independent universe.

A tradition sprang up in about the second year, whereby the audience members—all 1,200 of them—spend the entire evening wafting paper airplanes at the stage, and the people on stage spend the evening wafting them right back. The volume of paper dropping onto the stage is so great that we detail two people to constantly sweep away detritus; without them it would be nigh impossible to get about the stage.

The evening begins with the traditional Welcome, Welcome speech, delivered by an elderly matriarch and comprising in its entirety the statement, "Welcome, welcome." There is a grand and motley entrance parade of audience delegations such as the Museum of Bad Art; Lawyers For and Against Complexity; the Society for the Preservation of Slide Rules; the Junior Scientists' Club (all of whose members are about seven years old); Fruitcakes for a Better Tomorrow; the Society of Bearded Men; the Harvard Bureaucracy Club; Grannies Against Gravity; and the protest group Non-Extremists for Moderate Change in Finland.

At some point in the evening comes the Win-a-Date-with-a-Nobel-Laureate Contest, in which one lucky audience member wins a date with a Nobel Laureate.

The 1994 ceremony included the world premiere and only performance of *The Interpretive Dance of the Electrons*, a ballet performed by the Nicola Hawkins Dance Company and co-starring Nobel Laureates Richard Roberts, Dudley Herschbach, and William Lipscomb.

Every year since 1996 we have written a mini-opera that was then performed by professional opera singers and several Nobel Laureates. The key to making these operas work is to cast them with a mix of performers, all of whom are either (a) extremely skilled and talented or (b) endearingly game. *The Cockroach Opera* was our first. Later years saw the premieres of *Il Kaboom Grosso* (about the Big Bang, with a denouement featuring five Nobel Laureates as subatomic particles), *The Seedy Opera* (starring five tenors playing the role of Ig Nobel Prize–winning physicist Richard Seed, the man who plans to clone himself), *The Jargon Opera*, and other musical delights.

Each year's ceremony also includes some special event in which celebrities from the worlds of science, literature, and art get to show off unexpected talents.

The Heisenberg Certainty Lectures (named after the famous

Heisenberg Uncertainty Principle, which was named after Nobel Laureate Wehrner Heisenberg) have given many renowned scientists, university presidents, actors, politicians, and musicians the opportunity to lecture the audience on any topic they wished, with no restrictions save one. Each Heisenberg Lecturer was strictly limited to 30 seconds, with the time limit enforced by a professional baseball umpire. Anyone who exceeded the time limit was thrown off the stage. This proved popular with the audience.

One year, a collection of celebrated thinkers engaged in a contest to determine which of them is the world's smartest person. This was decided in a series of one-on-one, 30-second-long debates in which both debaters had to talk at the same time. Here, too, our referee, Mr. John Barrett, enforced the time limit.

At both the Sixth and Seventh First Annual Ig Nobel Prize Ceremonies, we auctioned off plaster casts of the (left) feet of Nobel Laureates. The proceeds were donated to the science programs of local schools.

The Eleventh First Annual Ceremony culminated in a wedding—a genuine wedding—of two scientists. The wedding ceremony was 60 seconds long, with 1,200 guests, including four teary-eyed Nobel Laureates and 40 people wearing Josef Stalin masks (it's a long story), the whole thing televised live on the Internet. Ig Nobel Prize winner Buck Weimer, the inventor of airtight underwear with a replaceable charcoal filter that removes bad-smelling gases before they can escape, presented the newlyweds with pairs of the underwear and instructed them on its use. Late that night, as the bride's mother was leaving Sanders Theatre, she beamingly told everyone that "This wasn't exactly what I would have planned for my daughter . . . but it was even better."

Every year, with so much going on during the ceremony, and with so many people having to give speeches, we faced a severe problem: how to graciously stop anyone who couldn't or wouldn't keep it brief. Our success with the 30-second-long Heisenberg Certainty Lectures eventually led us to an overall solution, and in 1999 we introduced a great technical innovation called "Miss Sweetie Poo."

Miss Sweetie Poo is an exceptionally cute eight-year-old girl. Whenever Miss Sweetie Poo feels that a speaker has exceeded his or her allotted time, she walks up to the lectern, looks up at the speaker, and says, "Please stop. I'm bored. Please stop. I'm bored. Please stop. I'm bored." Miss Sweetie Poo keeps saying this until the speaker gives up.

Miss Sweetie Poo is *very* effective. Since she has been part of the show, the ceremony has been 40% briefer than it had been before. Miss Sweetie Poo is our greatest invention.

Press coverage of the Ig from virtually every country on earth has grown and grown, and we have tried to make it easy for people in distant places to get a glimpse of the ceremony. Every year since 1993, National Public Radio has broadcast the Ig across North America, and ever since the Fifth First Annual Ig, in 1995, we have telecast every ceremony live on the Internet. For several years our telecast engineer was Harvard graduate student and convicted felon Robert Tappan Morris, the man whose worm program brought down the entire Internet and made him the first celebrated cyberspace criminal. You can see video and other highlights at the *Annals of Improbable Research* Web site (*www.improbable.com*).

And you are invited to send in a nomination, should you happen to know someone deserving, for one of next year's Ig Nobel Prizes.

CONTROVERSY

The Igs have not been without controversy. In 1995, Sir Robert May, the chief scientific advisor to the British government, asked the organizers to stop giving Ig Nobel Prizes to British scientists—even when the scientists want to receive them. May sent two angry letters to the Ig Nobel Board of Governors, and later granted interviews to the press. The reaction was not what he was expecting. Typical was the following editorial, which appeared in the October 7, 1996, issue of the British science journal *Chemistry & Industry*. It is reprinted here with permission from *Chemistry & Industry*.

WE ARE AMUSED

Is Britain's chief scientific adviser, Robert May, a pompous killjoy? In his recently publicised criticism of the IgNobel awards, a well-established spoof of the Nobel Prizes, he appears only to confirm that the British scientific establishment takes itself far too seriously.

In an interview with the journal *Nature*, May warns that the IgNobels risk bringing 'genuine' scientific projects into counter-productive ridicule. They should focus on anti-science and pseudo-science, he suggests, 'while leaving serious scientists to get on with their work.' His pique stems from embarrassing media coverage given to UK food scientists after an award last year for their research on soggy cereal flakes.

Such whineing has several flaws. First, it is not for bureaucrats like May to determine which scientists are 'serious,' or to ask that some researchers be ignored because they are above being made fun of (they aren't—the good ones as well as the bad ones).

Secondly, the IgNobels are organised by academics, for academics—unlike the notorious Golden Fleece awards in the US, with which May compares the IgNobels. The IgNobels let science laugh at itself.

Thirdly, the work of genuinely 'serious' scientists will withstand transitory embarrassment at the hands of TV comics and tabloid newspapers—assuming, of course, that their work really is recognised as 'serious' by other scientists. If, under a sudden spotlight, some scientists have to spend much time and effort explaining to everyone why their work is worth funding, that is a good thing and should happen more often, not less.

Finally, May reportedly suggests that the IgNobel organiser should obtain winners' consent first. But the British scientists did agree to receive their award last year, which makes May's grumbling distinctly off-target. Furthermore, that particular award proved that media mischief can not be avoided by obtaining prior consent. As the IgNobel organiser, Marc Abrahams, has pointed out to May, 'there are few things, good or bad, that British tabloids and TV comedians do not ridicule.'

Far from making a convincing case for the pernicious effect of the IgNobels, May's misfire only makes him (and British science) look thin-skinned and humourless. He mistakes discomfort for disaster, and solemnity for seriousness. And he misunderstands the point, the process, and the pleasure of the awards. On this topic, scientists and others should reject this adviser's ill-advised views. Long may British scientists take their rightful places in the IgNobel honour roll.

The 1995 Prize that prompted May's complaint honored three Norwich scientists "for their rigorous analysis of soggy breakfast cereal, published in a report titled 'A Study of the Effects of Water Content on the Compaction Behaviour of Breakfast Cereal Flakes.'" That same year, Nick Leeson won a share of the Economics Prize for his role in bringing down Barings Bank.

The Robert May flap did not deter the Ig Nobel Board of Governors from giving full consideration to high achievers in the UK. Nor did it deter future winners from accepting their unusual place on the world stage.

In 1996, undaunted by the very public stance of his nation's chief science official, Robert Matthews of Aston University won and happily accepted the Physics Prize for demonstrating that toast often falls on the buttered side. In 1997, Harold Hillman of the University of Surrey won the Ig Nobel Peace Prize for his influential report "The Possible Pain Experienced During Execution by Different Methods." In 1998, three doctors from the Royal Gwent Hospital shared the Medicine Prize with the anonymous patient who was the subject of their cautionary medical report, "A Man Who Pricked His Finger and Smelled Putrid for 5 Years."

Indeed, the UK has produced at least one winner (and often more) every year since 1992. The pool of UK nominees for the Ig Nobel Prize is so deep that it could easily supply all ten winners every year.

But the same is true of many other nations. In the unending competition for Igs, reputation alone counts for nothing. No country can or should rely on the glories of its past accomplishments.

In 2002 a curiously sweet twist of fate occurred in the form of a special guest. The British newspaper *The Observer* described it in their report about that year's ceremony:

> The real surprise was the presence of Professor David King, the Government's chief scientific adviser. The UK science establishment has scorned the Ig Nobels. King's predecessor, Lord May, demanded UK scientists be dropped from consideration because success might harm their careers. He had become incensed by East Anglia University scientists who won an award for explaining why breakfast cereal becomes soggy.
>
> 'I don't want to be critical of Bob [May], but I think this is all good fun,' said King.
>
> In fact, many scientists believe the Ig Nobel is better at enhancing the reputation of science than its straight-laced counterpart.

By the way—on Christmas Eve of that same year, 2002, the Japanese public television network NHK broadcast a special program about the Ig Nobel Prizes. The producers later told us that the program drew a larger audience than anything else broadcast on the network that entire year.

HOW TO READ THIS BOOK

This book is meant to be read aloud, preferably in elevators for the edification of your fellow passengers. Trains, buses, subways, and waiting rooms are other good places.

If you work in a group that has a tedious weekly meeting, try reading one section each week as a means of drawing the meeting to an early conclusion. No one will want, or be able, to discuss schedules and budgets after they hear your reading.

If you are a teacher, read some of the sections aloud in class, either as inspiration or as real-life cautionary tales. (Please do *not* tell your students beforehand that you'll be reading something funny. Just read it deadpan—that way it's much more enjoyable and memorable for the students as, one by one, they catch on and *really* start paying attention.)

Do not read the entire book at one sitting, as it might render you too jazzed or too jaded to sleep for the next several days.

Each of the Ig Nobel Prize winners has a much deeper and more intriguing story than it was possible to tell in this book. Use the references to find further information.

Go to the *Annals of Improbable Research* Web site (*www. improbable.com*) for links to (in most cases) the winners' home pages, published work, and/or press clippings. There you will also find video of several of the Ig Nobel Prize ceremonies, and links to recordings of the annual Ig Nobel radio broadcast on National Public Radio's "Talk of the Nation/Science Friday with Ira Flatow" program.

We also publish, in the magazine (*AIR*), and in the free monthly E-mail newsletter (mini-*AIR*), news of the continuing adventures of past Ig Nobel Prize winners.

After reading the book, you might find it interesting to do two things. First, compare your impression of particular Ig winners with that of someone whose judgment with which you think you agree. The question "Which of these are commendable and which damnable?" may reveal unexpected differences of opinion and personality.

Second, peruse the appendix that lists the winners year-by-year. Pick any year. Muse for a few moments about what ideas may have been batted around when that crop of winners met each other at the Ig Nobel Ceremony and playfully talked about combining their work. The discussion at the 1999 ceremony, for one, was particularly inspired.

A final word before you begin: THESE PEOPLE AND THEIR ACHIEVEMENTS ARE REAL. If you have trouble believing that—and you will—then use the references and *go look it up yourself.* Then you'll see . . .

MEDICAL BREAKTHROUGHS

 The human body is always falling apart. Doctors and medical personnel labor mightily to stave off decrepitude or repair what is broken, infected, or just haywire. Sometimes it works, sometimes it doesn't. Sometimes it leads to an Ig Nobel Prize. Here are three of the medical achievements that have been so honored:

- Failure of Electric Shock Treatment for Rattlesnake Envenomation
- Nose Picking in Adolescents
- Elevator Music Prevents the Common Cold

Failure of Electric Shock Treatment for Rattlesnake Envenomation

THE OFFICIAL CITATION
THE IG NOBEL MEDICINE PRIZE

This prize is awarded in two parts. First, to Patient X, formerly of the US Marine Corps, valiant victim of a venomous bite from his pet rattlesnake, for his determined use of electroshock therapy: at his own insistence, automobile spark-plug wires were attached to his lip, and the car engine revved to 3,000 rpm for five minutes. Second, to Dr. Richard C. Dart of the Rocky Mountain Poison Center and Dr. Richard A. Gustafson of the University of Arizona Health Sciences Center, for their well-grounded medical report: "Failure of Electric Shock Treatment for Rattlesnake Envenomation."

Their report was published in _Annals of Emergency Medicine,_ vol. 20, no. 6, June 1991, pp. 659–61.

A former US Marine received a lesson on the theme "don't believe everything you read." The lesson involved his pet rattlesnake, a car, a too-cooperative friend, an ambulance, a helicopter, several liters of intravenous isotonic fluids, a battery of medications, and numerous medical personnel.

The man in question will be identified here as he is in the published medical report: "Patient X." Having already been bitten some 14 times by his poisonous pet snake, Patient X did his best, he thought, to take precautions against a possible unlucky 15th chomp.

Though rattlesnake bites can be deadly, there is a standard treatment—injection with a substance called "antivenin." This almost always works, provided that the patient gets a sufficient amount soon after the bite occurs. For reasons that may at one time have been clear to him, Patient X was intent on using an alternative treatment.

He had read accounts in men's magazines of a powerful alternative treatment: application of a good, strong electric shock. High voltage was said to be essential. Some pundits recommended using an electric stun gun, and at least one company offered stun guns specially optimized for the purpose. Patient X and his friend agreed that, in the future, should either of them suffer a rattlesnake bite, the other would spring to the rescue with a bracing dose of electricity.

This ounce of prevention was worse than a pound of cure. Quite a bit worse.

One day, whilst Patient X was playing with his snake, the serpent embedded its fangs into Patient X's upper lip.

Patient X's friend immediately sprang into action. As per their agreement, he laid Patient X on the ground next to an automobile. He then connected Patient X to the car's electrical system, affixing a spark-plug wire to the stricken man's lip with a small metal clip.

The friend then revved the car engine to 3,000 rpm. To ensure a sufficient dose of electricity, he maintained that level for five minutes. As described in the medical report that was eventually published:

"The patient lost consciousness with the first electrical charge. An ambulance arrived approximately 15 minutes later to find the patient unconscious and incontinent of stool."

The ambulance attendants summoned a helicopter. During the flight, Patient X, rousing himself to some level of consciousness, fought off efforts to treat him.

A photograph taken shortly after he arrived at the hospital shows "massive swelling of face extending onto chest and ecchymosis of periorbital and upper chest regions." The man resembled a too-well-baked potato.

Dr. Richard Dart and Dr. Richard Gustafson, both then at the Arizona Poison and Drug Information Center at the University of Arizona Health Sciences Center, in Tucson, were brought onto the case. The treatment was complex and lengthy.

Of their patient's initial choice of treatment, Drs. Dart and Gustafson commented that:

"Despite many attempts, investigators in the United States have been unable to demonstrate any beneficial effect from electric shock treatment, even when applied under ideal conditions . . . In addition, this treatment may have adverse effects."

Eventually, with a substantial amount of medical help and despite his own earnest efforts, the patient made a full recovery. Dr. Dart and Dr. Gustafson wrote an instructive technical account of the case, which they published in the *Annals of Emergency Medicine.*

For educating the public about treatments for snakebite, Patient X and the two doctors who saved his life shared the 1994 Ig Nobel Prize in the field of Medicine.

The winners could not travel to the Ig Nobel Prize Ceremony, but Dr. Dart sent a tape-recorded acceptance speech. In accepting the Prize he said:

"I was stunned to receive this prize, although not as stunned as our patient."

The Dart/Gustafson medical report changed the way public health officials behave in regions where rattlesnakes abound. Public information campaigns now routinely include one extra item on their list of "Do Nots." An advisory from the Oklahoma Poison Control Center is typical. The list concludes with these items:

- **Do not** waste time capturing or killing the snake. Identification is helpful but not necessary.
- **Do not** apply a tourniquet.
- **Do not** pack wound in ice or apply heat.
- **Do not** give the victim a sedative or alcohol.
- **Do not** use a stun gun or electric shocks.

NOSE PICKING IN ADOLESCENTS

THE OFFICIAL CITATION

THE IG NOBEL PUBLIC HEALTH PRIZE WAS AWARDED TO

Chittaranjan Andrade and B.S. Srihari of the National Institute of Mental Health and Neurosciences, Bangalore, India, for their probing medical discovery that nose picking is a common activity among adolescents.

Their report was published as "A Preliminary Survey of Rhinotillexomania in an Adolescent Sample," *Journal of Clinical Psychiatry*, vol. 62, no. 6, June 2001, pp. 426–31.

As the 21st century arrived, two distinguished psychiatrists offered mankind proof—written proof—that most teenagers pick their noses.

Dr. Chittaranjan Andrade and Dr. B.S. Srihari, colleagues at the National Institute of Mental Health and Neurosciences in Bangalore, India, were inspired by an earlier published report by scientists in the American state of Wisconsin. The Wisconsin research claimed that more than 90% of adults are active nose pickers, but it was silent on the question of whether teenagers are less picky, as picky, or more picky than their elders.

Dr. Andrade and Dr. Srihari decided to find out. They had a serious purpose. Virtually any human activity, if carried to excess, can be considered a psychiatric disorder, and nose picking is no exception. "While nose-picking behaviour in general appears to be a common and normal habit," they wrote, "it is necessary to determine the extent to which rhinotillexomania amounting to a disorder exists in the adolescent population."

They prepared themselves by reading other medical reports about nose picking. With few exceptions, those reports dealt with spectacular individual nose pickers, most of whom were psychotic. Dr. Andrade and Dr. Srihari learned that nose picking, as practiced by disturbed individuals, can be chronic, violent, and associated with nose bleeds. The two psychiatrists studied Gigliotti and Waring's 1968 report, "Self-Inflicted Destruction of Nose and Palate: Report of Case." They scoured Akhtar and Hastings's 1978 report, "Life-Threatening Self-Mutilation of the Nose." They marveled at Tarachow's 1966 report, "Coprophagia and Allied Phenomena," noting from it that "persons do eat nasal debris, and find it tasty, too."

Those cases all had their points of interest, but they could serve only as background material for the work Drs. Andrade and Srihari had in mind. To determine the nose picking who, what, where, when, why, and how of a community, one must statistically sample the picking practices of many individuals.

Sampling is what the Wisconsin researchers did with adults. Sampling is what Drs. Andrade and Srihari knew they must do with adolescents.

They prepared a written survey that included the questions opposite. (You might enjoy taking this survey yourself, or applying it to friends and colleagues.)

For their careful, scholarly, and compulsively humane approach to the study of nose picking, Chittaranjan Andrade and B.S. Srihari were awarded the 2001 Ig Nobel Prize in the field of Public Health.

Dr. Andrade traveled from Bangalore, India, to Cambridge, Massachusetts, at his own expense, to attend the ceremony. In accepting the Prize, he said:

"On behalf of myself and on behalf of everybody else who is happy for me today, I'm happy to accept this year's Ig Nobel Prize in public health. My work was on . . . you won't believe it, just hold your breath—rhinotillexomania, which is a very fancy way of saying compulsive nose picking.

"Now, as you all know, having been adolescents yourself at some time, you've done things which were habitual, and I hope you haven't done things that were psychiatrically habitual such as trichotillomania, which means compulsive pulling of the hair, onychophagia, which means compulsive nail-biting, or rhinotillexiomania.

"Some people poke their nose into other people's business. I made it my business to poke my business into other people's noses. Thank you, folks."

Two days later, Dr. Andrade gave a public lecture and demonstration at the Ig Informal Lectures, elucidating the finer points of his research. In response to several questions, he assured anxious audience members that nose picking, in moderation, is "perfectly normal."

The *Times of India*, that nation's most prominent newspaper, reported the news on its front page with the headline "Ig Nobel for Indian Scientists Who Dig Deep."

Here are some questions from the survey:
- **In your opinion, what percentage of persons in the population pick their noses?**
- **On average, how often in a day do you pick your nose?**
- **Do you sometimes pick your nose in public? (please answer YES or NO)**
- **Why do you pick your nose? (please tick as many as are applicable to you)**
  - **To unclog your nasal passages**
  - **To relieve discomfort or itch**
  - **For cosmetic reasons**
  - **For personal hygiene**
  - **Out of habit**
  - **For pleasure**
- **How do you pick your nose? (please tick as many as are applicable to you)**
  - **Using your fingers**
  - **Using an object such as tweezers**
  - **Using an object such as a pencil**

(*continued*)

- Do you occasionally eat the nasal matter that you have picked? (please answer YES or NO)
- Do you consider that you have a serious nose-picking problem? (please answer YES or NO)

Some 200 students answered the survey.
The results showed some surprising things.
- Nose-picking practices are the same for all social classes.
- Less than 4% of the students claimed they never pick their noses. Half of the students pick their noses four or more times a day. About 7% say they indulge 20 or more times a day.
- 80% use their fingers exclusively. The rest are split almost evenly in their use of tools, some choosing tweezers while others prefer pencils.
- More than half said they do it to unclog nasal passages or relieve discomfort or itching. About 11% claimed they do it for cosmetic reasons, and a similar number do it just for pleasure.
- 4.5% said they ate the nasal debris.

These figures are just highlights. The survey produced a wealth of data.

ELEVATOR MUSIC PREVENTS THE COMMON COLD

THE OFFICIAL CITATION
THE IG NOBEL MEDICINE PRIZE WAS AWARDED TO

Carl J. Charnetski and Francis X. Brennan, Jr., of Wilkes University, and James F. Harrison of Muzak Ltd. in Seattle, Washington, for their discovery that listening to elevator Muzak stimulates immunoglobulin A (IgA) production, and thus may help prevent the common cold.

Their research report was published, a year after they won the Ig Nobel Prize, as "Effect of Music and Auditory Stimuli on Secretory Immunoglobulin A (IgA)," *Perceptual and Motor Skills*, vol. 87, no. 3, part 2, December 1998, pp. 1163–70.

Can music juice up your immune system? Can frequent sex? Several years ago, psychology professor Carl Charnetski attended a meeting where he heard someone mention a chemical called "immunoglobulin A." Professor Charnetski immediately began an ambitious research program that, so far, has involved immunoglobulin A, music, journalists, sex, and the spit of many persons.

Prophetically for Professor Charnetski, immunoglobulin A is also called "IgA." This chemical is one of many different so-called antibodies that the human immune system produces in response to infections or other dangers. Professor Charnetski reasoned that if he could find some common, pleasurable activity that causes the body to produce more of this chemical, he would have discovered an almost magical key to good health.

He and fellow professor Francis Brennan started looking for pleasurable activities that might have this effect. It would be easy to recognize, because someone's immunoglobulin A level is easy to measure—a saliva test is all it takes.

The first pleasurable activity they tested: listening to music. The research was simple. They had volunteers listen to music, and spit.

In the earliest experiments, they had college students listen to musical notes. The students heard 30 minutes of upbeat, cheery notes. Then they heard 30 minutes of downbeat, melancholy notes. The cheery music produced higher immunoglobulin A levels in the students' spit, but the dreary music produced lower levels.

Professors Charnetski and Brennan found this encouraging. Next, they teamed up with James Harrison of Muzak, Ltd—the company that produces much of the world's elevator music—to do an experiment using more familiar kinds of music.

They tested four groups of people:

- One group listened to a 30-minute tape recording of so-called environmental music, the kind of music some people call "smooth jazz."
- Another group listened to that same kind of music, but played from a radio instead of a tape.
- The third group listened to a half-hour of tones and clicking sounds.
- The fourth group was, in the researchers' words, "subjected to 30 minutes of silence."

The researchers tested everybody's spit.

Those who listened to smooth jazz from a tape recording had increased immunoglobulin A levels in their spit—but those who listened to it on the radio did not.

The tones-and-clicks listeners' spit contained *decreased* levels of immunoglobulin A.

Those who were "subjected to silence," like those who listened to smooth jazz on the radio, had unchanged spit.

Charnetski, Brennan, and Harrison announced that these findings were "significant" and could usher in a new era in the prevention of illness. For their harmonized attack on the common cold, Carl J. Charnetski, Francis X. Brennan, Jr., and James F. Harrison were awarded the 1997 Ig Nobel Prize in Medicine.

After mulling it over for a while, the winners decided that they could not, or would not, attend the Ig Nobel Prize Ceremony.

The team's research activities continued apace, although Harrison quietly dropped out of the picture.

Professors Charnetski and Brennan next explored how music affects the spit of newspaper reporters. That research was conducted on ten journalists in the newsroom of the Wilkes-Barre *Times Leader*. The results were encouraging, or at least suggestive, though perhaps not conclusive. (Full details are in the report "Stress and Immune System Function in a Newspaper's Newsroom," which appeared in the journal *Psychological Reports*.)

At that point, Professors Charnetski and Brennan switched their focus from music to sex. In 1999, they announced that college students who engage in frequent sexual intercourse have stronger immune systems than do those who mate less frequently.

Two years later, they summarized all of their research in a book called *Feeling Good Is Good for You*. The publisher's promotional blurb sums it up nicely:

"The media love to report how sex, laughter, and other simple pleasures are good for you. And you love to hear it. But is inciting pleasure a legitimate medical prescription for boosting a person's immunity? Can you literally fight off infection with a smile? Researchers Carl Charnetski and Francis Brennan say yes."

PSYCHOLOGY & INTELLIGENCE

 Psychologists study how people behave. People behave in unexpected ways. Sometimes, so do the psychologists studying them. Here are two examples:

- A Forbidding Experiment: Spitting, Chewing Gum, and Pigeons
- Ignorance Is Bliss

A Forbidding Experiment: Spitting, Chewing Gum, and Pigeons

THE OFFICIAL CITATION
THE IG NOBEL PSYCHOLOGY PRIZE WAS AWARDED TO

Lee Kuan Yew, former prime minister of Singapore, practitioner of the psychology of negative reinforcement, for his 30-year study of the effects of punishing four million citizens of Singapore whenever they spat, chewed gum, or fed pigeons.

While professional psychologists struggle to conduct their experiments on small groups of people, one dedicated, if uncredentialed, amateur psychologist tries out his theories on four million people at a time.

The populace of an entire country—Singapore—was banned from spitting, chewing gum, or feeding pigeons. These are the highlights of a many-fronted campaign to change people's trivial behaviors, and to do it in the way earlier psychologists trained rats, relying on punishment rather than persuasion.

The prohibitions were conceived and mandated by Lee Kuan Yew, the nation's former prime minister. Lee proudly, publicly, stated: "I think that a country has greater need of discipline than democracy." In Singapore, the discipline now covers a wide range of behavior.

Lee explained to a reporter that most Singaporean spitters are (like Lee himself) of Chinese descent:

"You know, the Chinese they spit everywhere. If you go to China, you can see them. And we started this very early. We say this is no good. This is a Third World habit. You spread tuberculosis, you spread all kinds of bad germs and diseases. So, we started with the school children, educated them, mass media and got the message home to the parents. And then we fine people. After they have been educated, they still do it, we fine them. And slowly, it has subsided."

On the global stage, Lee's antispitting campaign is not unprecedented, but it has two special twists.

In the late 19th and early 20th centuries, the US and other nations waged campaigns against spitting. These were part of a broader effort to halt the spread of tuberculosis, and for the most part relied on public relations, not legal sanctions. Lee Kuan Yew's Singapore sputum law has a little to do with public health, but a very lot to do with propriety. Jet-setters do not spit. And where other nations had announced that spitting is a crying shame, Lee Kuan Yew's Singapore decreed that spitting is a shaming crime.

In January 1992, the Singaporean government banned the manufacture, import, or sale of chewing gum. Officially, the new law was a matter of public tidiness. Journalists, though, discovered that it was actually a response to a single incident in which someone used a wad of chewing gum to jam the door sensor of a subway car.

To Lee Kuan Yew and his government, pigeons are as undesirable, as abominable, as rats. The Singapore Housing and Development Board give the official explanation:

"Pigeons and crows visit the town because of the food left by residents. Birds can bring with them certain health risks and nuisance such as food poisoning. In addition, the droppings of birds can soil the laundry, cars, walls and floors, and damage roof tiles."

Throughout Singapore, pigeon feeding was deemed not just undesirable, but impermissible.

In the aforementioned interview with the Japanese television network, Lee explained that he has been trying to "make this Third World country into a First World oasis." Buildings and roads, he said, are the straightforward part of that. But "[it's] very difficult, to change Third World habits into First World habits. So, it has to be through a long process of education."

In yanking his country's economy and social structure forward, Lee Kuan Yew has dared to tinker with conventional educational theory. In other parts of the world, education is not yet so straight-forwardly based on fining, jailing, or (as with many Singapore laws) beating people.

As prime minister, and then in his role of power behind the throne, Lee has mounted many campaigns, against spitting, gum-chewing and pigeon-feeding, yes—but also against littering, smoking, and foul language. And he has pressed hard in favor of some of his favorite things: smiling, being courteous, and the scrupulous flushing of public toilets.

For his commanding research on how people ought to behave, Lee Kuan Yew won the 1994 Ig Nobel Prize in the field of Psychology.

The winner could not, or would not, attend the Ig Nobel Prize Ceremony.

IGNORANCE IS BLISS

THE OFFICIAL CITATION

THE IG NOBEL PSYCHOLOGY PRIZE WAS AWARDED TO

David Dunning of Cornell University and Justin Kruger of the University of Illinois, for their modest report, "Unskilled and Unaware of It: How Difficulties in Recognizing One's Own Incompetence Lead to Inflated Self-Assessments."

Their study was published in the _Journal of Personality and Social Psychology,_ vol. 77, no. 6, December 1999, pp. 1121–34.

Everyone is incompetent, one way or another. David Dunning and Justin Kruger collected scientific evidence that incompetence is bliss.

Dunning and Kruger wanted to explore the breadth and depth of human incompetence. They staged a series of experiments at Cornell University involving several groups of people. Before commencing the experimentation, they made some predictions, most notably:

1. That incompetent people dramatically overestimate their ability; and
2. That incompetent people are not good at recognizing incompetence—their own or anyone else's.

In one experiment, Dunning and Kruger tested people's ability to tell whether jokes are funny—specifically, their ability to tell whether other people would laugh at the jokes.

They prepared a list of jokes. These jokes spanned a range from the officially Not Very Funny ("Question: What is as big as a man, but weighs nothing? Answer: His shadow.") to the officially Very Funny ("If a kid asks where rain comes from, I think a cute thing to tell him is 'God is crying.' And if he asks why God is crying, another cute thing to tell him is 'probably because of something you did.'").

Dunning and Kruger then asked 65 test subjects to rate the funniness of each joke. They showed the same jokes to a panel of eight professional comedians—people who, as Dunning and Kruger point out, "make their living by recognizing what is funny and reporting it to their audiences." They then compared each test subject's ratings of the jokes with those of the professional comedians.

Some people had a very poor sense of what others find funny—but most of those same individuals believed themselves to be very good at it.

Dunning and Kruger realized that a sense of humor can be a tricky thing to judge, so their next experiment used tests that are easier to measure: logic questions from law-school entrance exams. The logic questions produced much the same results as jokes. Those with poor reasoning skills tended to believe they were the intellectual peers of Bertrand Russell or Mr. Spock.

Overall, the results showed that incompetence is even worse than it appears to be. Not only do incompetent people not recognize their own incompetence; they also don't recognize competence when they see it in other people.

David Dunning explained why he took up this kind of research: "I am interested in why people tend to have overly favorable and objectively indefensible views of their own abilities, talents, and moral character. For example, a full 94% of college professors state that they do 'above average' work, although it is statistically impossible for virtually everybody to be above average."

Dunning and Kruger are themselves college professors (though at the time they did the experiment, Kruger was still Dunning's student). When they published their final report, the concluding words showed a degree of modesty: "To the extent this article is imperfect, it is not a sin we have committed knowingly."

For celebrating incompetence and unawareness, David Dunning and Justin Kruger won the 2000 Ig Nobel Prize in the field of Psychology.

The winners could not, or would not—or at least did not—attend the Ig Nobel Prize Ceremony. It was and is unclear whether their absence was intentional.

Note: if you have colleagues who are incompetent and unaware of it, Dunning and Kruger's research is a useful and convenient tool. We recommend that you make photocopies of this report, and send them—anonymously, if need be—to each of those individuals. Repeat as necessary.

ECONOMICS

Almost everyone wants more money. Almost no one is quite sure how to get it.

Certain persons came up with startling economic insights that they apparently felt compelled to act upon. These people produced some memorable Ig Nobel Prize–winning achievements. Among them:

- Squeezing Orange County/Bringing Down Barings
- The Good Lloyd's Shepherds Insure Disaster
- Dying to Save Taxes
- Enron—and Then Some (and Then None)

Squeezing Orange County/Bringing Down Barings

THE OFFICIAL CITATION
THE IG NOBEL ECONOMICS PRIZE WAS . . .

Awarded jointly to Nick Leeson and his superiors at Barings Bank, and to Robert Citron of Orange County, California, for using the calculus of derivatives to demonstrate that every financial institution has its limits.

For an introduction to the work and legacy of Nick Leeson, see the book *Rogue Trader: How I Brought Down Barings Bank and Shook the Financial World,* by Nick Leeson, Little, Brown, 1996.

For an introduction to the work and legacy of Robert Citron, see the book *Big Bets Gone Bad: Derivatives and Bankruptcy in Orange County,* by Philippe Jorion, Academic Press, 1995.

1. Risk can be profitable!
2. Risk can be exciting!
3. Risk can be risky!
 . . .

 . . .
 86. Risk can be disastrous.

This succession of thoughts, or one much like it, may have occurred to both Robert Citron and Nick Leeson as each whiled away his time in prison. Each man had taken a series of risky gambles with other people's money, and found disaster beyond his wildest dreams.

These were two scandals of nearly mythic import, occurring one on the heels of the other. Thanks to Citron, one of America's wealthiest counties (were it a nation, Orange County would have been the 30th largest in the world) suddenly went bust. Thanks to Leeson, one of England's oldest banks suddenly went bankrupt.

Robert Citron and Nick Leeson made bold investments, buying and selling things called "derivatives."

What is a derivative? Well, the definition wasn't so important—it appears that neither Citron nor Leeson really understood what a derivative is. What mattered was that each man had tremendous self-confidence—and tremendous self-confidence is the hallmark of the born financial genius. Both men had been hailed as true geniuses, because for a while each had brought staggering success.

Robert Citron was the treasurer of Orange County, California. He invested (or as some would later say, "gambled") the county's money in stocks and derivatives. At first, he was very skilled (or lucky), and made fantastically huge profits.

Nick Leeson was a trader in the Singapore office of Barings Bank, one of Britain's most venerable institutions. He "invested" the bank's money in stocks and derivatives. At first he was very "skilled" and made fantastically huge profits.

In October 1994, Citron's investments all went completely sour. Orange County went bankrupt.

In February 1995, Leeson's investments all went completely sour. Barings Bank collapsed.

After things blew up, supervisors at Barings and in Orange County expressed great surprise. The financial press delighted in describing these parallel catastrophes. A 1996 report from *Bloomberg Business News* put it pithily:

"Regulators who have picked up the pieces from similar disasters—from Nick Leeson's $1.4 billion of losses for Barings PLC to Robert Citron's $1.7 billion of losses for Orange County, Calif.—say the fallout generally follows a familiar pattern: the institution blames a lone trader. As more evidence develops, it becomes clear the losses stem as much from bosses who were willing to overlook trading risks as from the deceptions of an individual.

" 'Nobody calls you a rogue trader until you start losing money,' said Philip McBride Johnson, a Washington attorney who was chairman of the Commodities Futures Trading Commission from 1981 to 1983. 'It's amazing how people can do pretty much what they want as long as they make money.'

"Orange County supervisors, who were required by law to help oversee the county's finances, said they didn't understand Citron's investment strategy or the risks involved. Peter Norris, head of Barings's investment banking, said that none of the company's top managers actually understood the intricacies of derivatives trading."

Just days before Orange County filed for bankruptcy, Citron was forced to resign his post.

Just hours before Barings crashed, Leeson fled his office in Singapore. His first stop was Malaysia, then it was on to Brunei, Thailand, and finally Germany, where the police gave him accommodations in a lovely jail cell. After six months of spirited negotiation, Leeson was whisked back to Singapore for a rendezvous with the criminal justice system there.

Orange County went into bankruptcy. The remains of Barings Bank were sold, for the price of £1, to the Dutch banking and insurance company ING.

For their accomplishments, Robert Citron and Nick Leeson shared the 1995 Ig Nobel Prize in the field of Economics.

The winners could not, or would not, attend the Ig Nobel Prize Ceremony. Each had a previous engagement.

Citron had begun serving a five-year prison term (eventually reduced to one year). He revealed that in deciding where and how to invest Orange County's money, he had consulted not just Merrill Lynch and other large corporate financial advisers, but also a local psychic and a mail-order astrologer.

Leeson had begun serving a six-year stretch (eventually reduced to two years) in Tanah Merah prison, Changi, Singapore. While there, he coauthored a charming book called *Rogue Trader: How I Brought Down Barings Bank and Shook the Financial World*. The book ends as he is about to be extradited from Germany to Singapore. Leeson muses fondly about his former supervisors:

"I realized that I was glad to have played my part in this fiasco rather than theirs. I was happier in my prison cell than they were, sitting at home nursing their credibility back to pieces and always knowing what their friends were saying behind their backs. Fuck 'em! I thought."

Since emerging from prison, Leeson has gone on to the lecture circuit where, according to press accounts, he is paid as much as $100,000 to warn audiences about the need for tighter corporate controls and regulation.

THE GOOD LLOYD'S SHEPHERDS INSURE DISASTER

THE OFFICIAL CITATION
THE IG NOBEL ECONOMICS PRIZE WAS AWARDED TO

The investors of Lloyd's of London, heirs to 300 years of dull, prudent management, for their bold attempt to insure disaster by refusing to pay for their company's losses.

Several books try to describe the Lloyd's of London story. One is *Ultimate Risk: The Inside Story of the Lloyd's Catastrophe*, by Adam Raphael, Four Walls Eight Windows, 1995.

Over the span of three centuries, Lloyd's of London became the biggest, most innovative, most influential, most respected, and most profitable insurance company in the world. Then, just like that, it was coming apart at the seams.

Lloyd's investors are obligated by law and sacred oath to personally pony up for the company's losses. During the first 300 years, Lloyd's almost always made a profit, but the moment that changed, most of those investors—including many of great wealth, power, and fame—refused to pay up. And that put the company into one hell of a spot.

A lot of people made a lot of very bad decisions.

Lloyd's of London has always been peculiarly organized, and, until the 1980s, it was peculiarly profitable. In its later years, Lloyd's became a mess, the kind of mess that is awkwardly draped atop a larger mess, a larger mess that is somehow supported by a more massive mess, a massive mess that manages to conceal within it a type of mess that beggars all description.

Until it blew up, Lloyd's of London was entirely owned by a select group of individuals known as the "Names." To be a "Name" was considered a privilege and an honor; only the wealthy and powerful were called. Unlike investors in other companies, the Names pledged to cede Lloyd's of London their own fortunes in the then unlikely event the company incurred losses. Happily, Lloyd's almost never incurred losses. Nearly every year brought nice fat profits, which the company parceled out to the little gaggle of Names.

'Twas a happy and seemingly perpetual arrangement. And then things changed. Rapidly. A series of natural disasters—Hurricane Betsy, the Exxon *Valdez* oil tanker spill, etc.—caused high losses. Many of the Names got angry, and threatened not to pay up.

Lloyd's managers scrambled to add new investors—lots of 'em. They loosened the company rules so that just about anyone, not just the rich, could become a Name. Suddenly Lloyd's had thousands of new Names. Many were Americans and Canadians who pledged their right arms—and their entire net worth, no matter how tiny—for the chance to (maybe, just maybe!) join the British upper crust. Where, in 1970, there had been 6,000 Names, most of them reasonably wealthy, by 1987, there were 30,000, many of them lower middle class.

When the company then incurred massive losses—£500 million in 1988, £2 billion in 1989, almost £3 billion the next year, many of the new Names were asked to fork over everything they owned. For them it had been "Welcome to Lloyd's, Welcome to Instant Bankruptcy!"

The situation was grim. Most refused to pay. Instead, they filed lawsuits.

But wait—there was more. Lloyd's management had done something clever. They'd gotten the government to exempt Lloyd's from many of the nation's basic financial rules, making it difficult for the Names to sue.

But wait—there was more. Under Lloyd's bizarre accounting rules, the ruined Names owed the company not just everything they owned at the moment, but also much of their earnings in the future. And no one could say how much they would still owe in the future. No one could even say if there would ever be a limit to the amount. And if the ruined Names were to die, the obligations would then fall upon their children.

And was there more? Of course there was. In the cozy, traditional Lloyd's way of arranging things, many of the older, wealthier Names and some of the better-connected new Names were *not* asked to pay anything.

More? Glad you asked. Many of the older Names resented the pleadings of those who were ruined, and made a big point of not helping them. *Noblesse* not *oblige*.

For the whole sad, twisted mess, the Names of Lloyd's of London won the 1992 Ig Nobel Prize in the field of Economics.

The winners could not, or would not, attend the Ig Nobel Prize Ceremony.

New lawsuits popped up all over the place. The list of Names shriveled—by the year 2001, there were fewer than 3,000 individuals left. Lloyd's did manage to keep its institutional nostrils above water; they did it by selling stock to corporate investors, savvy businesses that refused to accept the romantic pledge-your-every-last-iota requirement. As to the future: no one can say for how long Lloyd's famous bell will continue to toll, or for whom.

DYING TO SAVE TAXES

THE OFFICIAL CITATION
THE IG NOBEL ECONOMICS PRIZE WAS AWARDED TO
Joel Slemrod of the University of Michigan Business School, and Wojciech Kopczuk of the University of British Columbia, for their conclusion that people find a way to postpone their deaths if that would qualify them for a lower rate on the inheritance tax.

Their report was published as "Dying to Save Taxes: Evidence from Estate Tax Returns on the Death Elasticity," *National Bureau of Economic Research Working Paper No. W8158,* **March 2001.**

By doing some intense, skillful detective work, Joel Slemrod and Wojciech Kopczuk found evidence that people will do pretty much anything for money—even die for it.

Economists like to believe that people make rational decisions and base all their actions on cool, self-interested thought. In the backs of their minds, though, they wonder.

Joel Slemrod wondered quite a bit, and he asked a simple question that few economists had dared to raise:

"Could the timing of death be, to some extent, a *rational* decision? Economists presume that the timing of other important events, such as childbearing or marriage, may be so affected—why not dying itself?"

Being a professor of business economics and public policy, and director of the Office of Tax Policy Research at the University of

Michigan, Slemrod knew how to seek the answer. Together with his prize graduate student Wojciech Kopczuk, he sifted through nearly a century's worth of tax records.

Other economists had dug into the slightly less existential questions of whether people time their marriage ceremonies to take advantage of tax laws, or whether they time the conception and birth of their children to maximize the tax benefits. "If birth," Slemrod and Kopczuk asked, "why not death?"

The idea of timing one's exit had been looked into, at least slightly, by physicians. Medical libraries are full of reports analyzing when and how people tiptoe off life's stage. (One called "Postponement of Death Until Symbolically Meaningful Occasions," published in 1990 in the *Journal of the American Medical Association*, claims that the death rate "dips before a symbolically meaningful occasion" such as a big religious holiday, "and peaks just afterward.")

Many countries impose a tax on those who inherit substantial possessions. It goes under different names—inheritance tax, estate tax, death tax, etc. Exactly what is taxed and at what rate varies considerably from nation to nation, in some cases from locality to locality, and in many cases from one year to another.

In the US, where Slemrod and Kopczuk live and work, the first such tax of real consequence was instituted in 1916. Under various political pressures, the rate bounced up and down quite often. Slemrod and Kopczuk looked at what happened when the estate tax rate increased markedly on eight occasions (twice in 1917, and once each in 1924, 1932, 1934, 1935, 1940, and 1941) and decreased on five others (in 1919, 1926, 1942, 1983, and 1984).

The analysis was complex, but it all boiled down to a simple conclusion:

"There is abundant evidence that some people will themselves to survive in order to live through a momentous event. Evidence from estate tax returns suggests that some people will themselves to survive a bit longer if it will enrich their heirs."

Slemrod and Kopczuk are modest about their work. "To be sure," they say, "the evidence is not overwhelming." They also mention the possibility that, in some cases, relatives intentionally report an incorrect date of departure.

For their work, Joel Slemrod and Wojciech Kopczuk won the 2001 Ig Nobel Prize in the field of Economics.

Joel Slemrod traveled to the Ig Nobel Prize Ceremony, at his own expense. In accepting the Prize, he said:

"Well, never in my wildest dreams did I think it would be like this. I'm pleased to accept the Ig Nobel for myself and my coauthor, who I think is watching the video stream up in Vancouver. Also, I think my son and daughter are watching. Hi, kids. We are pleased to accept this award because we believe in the spirit of the Ig, that the pursuit of science, even social science, can be fun and that sometimes we learn by pushing our hypotheses into extreme and unlikely places. Our research provides evidence about something everybody already knows, that some people will do anything for money. Of course, other people live their whole lives with no regard for money, and sorting this out is a continuing challenge for economics.

"Little did we know that when we did this research, the US Congress, in its wisdom, would vote to abolish the US estate tax for the year 2010—and *only* the year 2010—setting up the best natural experiment for a hypothesis ever conceived. Somebody, I think maybe Benjamin Franklin, once said that the only two inevitable things are death and taxes. Well, come 2010, it will be death *or* taxes."

ENRON—AND THEN SOME (AND THEN NONE)

THE OFFICIAL CITATION
THE IG NOBEL ECONOMICS PRIZE WAS AWARDED TO

The executives, corporate directors, and auditors of Enron, Lernout & Hauspie [Belgium], Adelphia, Bank of Commerce and Credit International [Pakistan], Cendant, CMS Energy, Duke Energy, Dynegy, Gazprom [Russia], Global Crossing, HIH Insurance [Australia], Informix, Kmart, Maxwell Communications [UK], McKessonHBOC, Merrill Lynch, Merck, Peregrine Systems, Qwest Communications, Reliant Resources, Rent-Way, Rite Aid, Sunbeam, Tyco, Waste Management, WorldCom, Xerox, and Arthur Andersen, for adapting the mathematical concept of imaginary numbers for use in the business world. [Note: all companies are US-based unless otherwise noted.]

Imaginary numbers used to be dull, mathematical things, but that's changing. A group of imaginative business leaders gave new life—and

The full, detailed stories of each of these co-winners (as much as has been made public, at least) is extensively reported in most of the world's major newspapers, magazines, and other news media, as well as in an ever-growing collection of books. Further details await your scrutiny in court documents in numerous jurisdictions on several continents.

then some—to the old, engineering definition of "imaginary numbers." So, now there are two definitions. The engineers, in their staid belief that reliability somehow matters, still base theirs on the square root of the number "minus one." The business executives, with an eye to the future, base theirs on hopes and dreams and press releases.

Numbers became very exciting in the 1980s and 1990s, even to people who hate math. Here are some of the most thrilling numbers that got imagined during that period:

Enron, an energy company, announced in the year 2001 that $591 million of its income was imaginary.

Lernout & Hauspie, a speech technology company, announced in the year 2001 that more than $100 million of its revenue was imaginary.

Adelphia, a cable television company, announced in the year 2002 that $1.6 billion of its finances was imaginary.

Bank of Commerce and Credit International, a bank, announced in the year 1991 that $600 million of its finances was imaginary.

Cendant, a car rental, hotel, and real estate company, announced in the year 1998 that $500 million of its income was imaginary.

CMS Energy Corp., an energy company, announced in the year 2001 that $4.2 billion of its revenue was imaginary, then a few months later announced that an additional billion dollars was imaginary.

Duke Energy, an energy company, announced in the year 2002 that $217 million of its revenue was imaginary.

Dynegy, an energy company, announced in the year 2002 that $300 million of its income was imaginary.

Gazprom, a Russian gas company, announced nothing. Press reports explained that several billion dollars of Gazprom's finances was imaginary.

Global Crossing, a telecommunications company, announced in the year 2002 that, although it had an imaginary valuation of $55 billion, the firm would file for bankruptcy and its investors would likely get nothing.

HIH Insurance, based in Australia, announced in the year 2002 that $930 million of its funding was imaginary.

Informix, a software company, announced in the year 1997 that $295 million of its revenue was imaginary.

Kmart, a department store chain, announced in the year 2002 that $501 million of its revenue was imaginary.

Maxwell Communications, a news media company, announced in the year 1991 that £400 million of its pension fund was imaginary.

McKessonHBOC, a health-care supply and services company, announced in the year 1999 that $42.2 million of its revenue was imaginary.

Merrill Lynch, a stockbroking company, announced in the year 2002 that it would pay $100 million in fines to the New York State government because many of its financial numbers were imaginary.

Merck, a pharmaceuticals company, announced in the year 2002 that $12.4 billion of its revenue was imaginary.

Peregrine Systems, a software company, announced in the year 2002 that $100 million of its revenue was imaginary.

Qwest Communications, a telecommunications company, announced in the year 2002 that $950 million of its revenue was imaginary, and that a further $531 million, also, might be imaginary.

Reliant Resources, an energy company, announced in the year 2002 that $6.4 billion of its revenue was imaginary.

Rent-Way, a rent-to-own chain of stores, announced in the year 2001 that $127 million of its revenue was imaginary.

Rite Aid, a drugstore chain, announced in the year 2002 that $1.6 billion of its revenue was imaginary.

Sunbeam, an electrical appliance manufacturing company, announced in the year 2002 that $44 million of its revenue was imaginary.

Tyco International Ltd., a technology conglomerate, announced in the year 2002 that $101.4 million of its revenue was imaginary.

Waste Management, a waste disposal company, announced in the year 2000 that $3.5 billion of its finances was imaginary.

WorldCom, a telecommunications company, announced in the year 2002 that $7.6 billion of its revenue was imaginary, and that a further $2 billion, also might be imaginary.

Xerox, a photocopier and computer technology company, announced in the year 2002 that $6.4 billion of its revenue was imaginary.

Arthur Andersen, an accounting firm, announced in the year 2002 that many of the financial statements of many of its biggest clients (including several of the companies mentioned here) were imaginary.

Many other companies joined in on the fun, but the ones mentioned here were the most celebrated.

For adding two and two, and getting four billion, the executives, corporate directors, and auditors of Enron, Lernout & Hauspie, Adelphia, Bank of Commerce and Credit International, Cendant, CMS Energy, Duke Energy, Dynegy, Gazprom, Global Crossing, HIH Insurance, Informix, Kmart, Maxwell Communications, McKesson-HBOC, Merrill Lynch, Merck, Peregrine Systems, Qwest Communications, Reliant Resources, Rent-Way, Rite Aid, Sunbeam, Tyco, Waste Management, WorldCom, Xerox, and Arthur Andersen shared the 2002 Ig Nobel Prize in the field of Economics.

The winners could not, or would not, attend the Ig Nobel Prize Ceremony.

At the ceremony, as the list of Economics Prize co-winners was announced (a process that inevitably took several minutes), and as a man and women dressed in expensive business suits shredded documents on stage, the audience was, as one, applauding and roaring with a rather frightening degree of fervor.

PEACE—DIPLOMACY AND PERSUASION

 Masters of diplomacy and peacemaking are, in some cases, highly idiosyncratic. Here are three outstanding examples:

- The Levitating Crime Fighters
- Daryl Gates, the Gandhi of Los Angeles
- Stalin World

THE LEVITATING CRIME FIGHTERS

THE OFFICIAL CITATION
THE IG NOBEL PEACE PRIZE WAS AWARDED TO
John Hagelin of Maharishi University and the Institute of Science, Technology and Public Policy, promulgator of peaceful thoughts, for his experimental conclusion that 4,000 trained meditators caused an 18% decrease in violent crime in Washington, DC.

His study was published as "Interim Report: Results of the National Demonstration Project to Reduce Violent Crime and Improve Governmental Effectiveness in Washington, DC, June 7 to July 30, 1993," Institute of Science, Technology and Public Policy, Fairfield, Iowa.

In June and July of 1993, a group of scientists performed a bold experiment.

Their aim: to drastically reduce the amount of violent crime in Washington, DC—a famous den of murder, rape, and robbery.

Their method: to scientifically and systematically blanket the city with the mental emanations from transcendental meditation and yogic flying.

John Hagelin is, by his own admission, a remarkable man. He is Professor of Physics and Director of the Institute of Science, Technology and Public Policy at the prestigious Maharishi University of Management, in Fairfield, Iowa. He is a practiced expert in quantum physics, transcendental meditation, yogic flying, and running for president of the US.

John Hagelin is very concerned about crime.

"As a Dartmouth- and Harvard-trained, unified-field theoretical physicist," he wrote in a letter to a newspaper, "I have been fortunate to have worked closely with the world's foremost scientist in the field of consciousness, Maharishi Mahesh Yogi. As a patriot and scientist, I am prepared to provide our government with the scientific knowledge and the proven, natural-law-based solutions to the problems that confront the nation."

John Hagelin is very concerned about crime.

In 1992, he was the Natural Law Party's candidate for president of the US. He was not elected that year. He ran again in 1996 and 2000. Records indicate that he was not elected in either of those years. The Natural Law Party is based at the Institute of Science, Technology and Public Policy at the prestigious Maharishi University of Management, in Fairfield, Iowa, and has branches in England, Germany, India, Switzerland, Thailand, Bermuda, Croatia, Latvia, Argentina, and some 70 other nations.

John Hagelin is very concerned about crime.

In 1993, he perfected a method for preventing violent crime.

In technical terms, the method consists of "forming coherence groups in major cities to lower the stress throughout our society, in order to alleviate the prime cause of criminality." In plain words: Hagelin pays people to meditate and levitate themselves off carpets. When a sufficient number of skilled people do this at the same time and in the same place, the crime rate drops. It's as simple as that.

He demonstrated this method in the summer of 1993. From June 7 through July 30, 4,000 trained meditators meditated and levitated themselves in and/or near Washington, DC.

At a press conference held a year later, just weeks before the presidential election, candidate John Hagelin announced the results of his experiment: it was a success. While the meditators were meditating and levitating, Washington's crime rate had dropped by 18%.

Technically speaking, that is. The rate of actual crimes committed in Washington did not drop by 18%—in fact, during the experiment, Washington's weekly murder rate hit the highest level ever recorded. However, the crime rate was 18% lower than what John Hagelin's

computer predicted it would have been had not 4,000 trained meditators been meditating and levitating.

For his influence on criminals, John Hagelin won the 1994 Ig
Nobel Peace Prize.

The winner could not, or would not, attend the Ig Nobel Prize
Ceremony.

In subsequent years, John Hagelin continued his experiments.
Early in 2001, Hagelin, together with the Maharishi Mahesh Yogi
and Indian Major General Kulwant Singh, held a news conference in
Washington, DC, to announce a fund-raising drive. The purpose: to
raise $1,000,000,000, the interest from which would pay for a squad
of 40,000 trained yogic levitators, who would patrol war zones and
thus bring peace to the world. They expressed confidence that they
could persuade people to invest in their plan.

And in the summer of 2002, Hagelin held a press conference to
inform all parties in the Middle East that peace would soon be
achieved there, once he and his trained meditators and levitators
swung into action, which would happen as soon as they received the
massive—but given the task at hand, modest—funding they desired.

DARYL GATES, THE GANDHI OF LOS ANGELES

THE OFFICIAL CITATION
THE IG NOBEL PEACE PRIZE WAS AWARDED TO

Daryl Gates, former police chief of the city of Los Angeles, for his uniquely compelling methods of bringing people together.

There are several books about the Rodney King riots and Chief Gates's role pertaining to them. One is *Official Negligence: How Rodney King and the Riots Changed Los Angeles and the LAPD,* by Lou Cannon, Times Books, 1997. Daryl Gates himself coauthored a book in which he to some degree addresses the subject: *Chief: My Life in the LAPD,* by Daryl F. Gates with Diane K. Shah, Bantam Books, 1992.

Daryl Gates ran the most publicized police force in history, an organization glorified in movies and books, and especially on television. Then, one day, TV stations began showing—and endlessly repeating— videotape of several police officers, all of whom were white, viciously beating a traffic violator who was black. The public demanded that the cops be punished. It was at this point that Chief Gates, using a charismatic blend of actions and pronouncements, inaction and silence, helped the small, nasty incident grow into something big and long-lived. In several parts of the city, aggrieved people came together and started rioting. Every shocking bit was televised, uniting the many peoples of the earth in voyeuristic revulsion.

In the wee hours of March 3, 1991, a group of Los Angeles police officers chased a very drunken man named Rodney King as he sped his car down a freeway. They caught him, and a week later, millions of television viewers watched videotape of the officers beating and beating and beating Rodney King with metal batons, and also kicking and stomping on him. Los Angeles is the television and movie capital of the universe and, by 1991, seemingly every Los Angelino owned a video camera. The man who taped the Rodney King beating was a neighbor who had been awakened by the sirens and the shouting, and who happened to have a brand-new camera he wanted to test out.

For decades, television shows such as *Dragnet, Columbo, Hunter,* and *Adam-12* broadcast attractive pictures of the Los Angeles Police Department (LAPD). The LA cops in these programs were always courteous and humane. The LA cops in the Rodney King video appeared to be quite something else.

The LAPD had always had a seamy, unpublicized side. Charges of police brutality—especially against black and Latino citizens—were so common that the city government expected to pay vast sums every year in legal settlements.

The Rodney King incident set the city's teeth on edge. Four of the cops were put on trial, charged with using excessive force. Having seen the videotape, the world expected them to be convicted of at least some of the charges. Everyone in Los Angeles feared, though, that if the jury somehow let the accused cops off the hook, rioting would erupt in the streets.

An all-white jury somehow *did* let the accused cops off the hook, and as the news spread across town, riots *did* erupt. These were the biggest riots the US had seen in more than two decades.

For years, Chief Gates had been bragging that his police force, having learned from past failures, was fully trained and fully prepared to cool any potential disturbance the moment it started. It turned out he was wrong.

Under Chief Gates's direction, or lack of direction, the LAPD was disorganized beyond disorganized and did almost nothing to quell the riots until it was far too late. Bizarrely, as people were being attacked and killed in the streets, and as buildings and cars were being torched, and as the world watched it all on television, Chief Gates left his post to attend a political fund-raising event. By the time he returned several hours later, things had gotten completely out of hand.

At the height of the troubles, Rodney King himself stepped back into the spotlight and played a curiously calming role. He went on television and plaintively asked, "Can't we all get along?"

Two months after the riots ended, with much of the public screaming for his head, Daryl Gates resigned as police chief of the city of Los Angeles. Although he had certainly not caused the troubles, his gritty determination and tough-guy posturing had helped bring thousands of riotous Los Angelenos and millions of television viewers together in ways they had never imagined.

For this, Daryl Gates won the 1992 Ig Nobel Peace Prize. The winner could not, or would not, attend the Ig Nobel Prize Ceremony. The Ig Nobel Board of Governors arranged for Mr. Stan Goldberg, manager of the Crimson Tech Camera Store in Cambridge, Massachusetts, to accept the Prize on behalf of Chief Gates. Here is the text of Mr. Goldberg's acceptance speech:

"As general manager of Crimson Tech Camera Store, I am pleased to accept this award on behalf of Daryl Gates. Daryl Gates has done more for the videocamera industry than any other individual. He has shown the world how a good-quality videocamera can capture the memories of a generation. [Here, Mr. Goldberg held up a videocamera.] Take this baby, for instance. It's a model VHS-C with one-lux light sensitivity, and AF power zoom/macro lens, full-range autofocus, and automatic time-date stamping. We sell it for just $599.98, which includes a free bonus case. We'll beat any competitor's advertised price . . ." (At this point several people rushed on stage, attacked Mr. Goldberg, and removed him from the building. It is believed that a member of the audience videotaped the incident and offered it for sale to the television networks.)

In July 1992, a very few months after resigning as police chief and just three months before being awarded the Ig Nobel Prize, Daryl Gates published a hastily written (well, co-written) autobiography, titling it *Chief: My Life in the LAPD*. The book's ending is as forthright and blunt as the man himself:

"By the beginning of 1992, I knew it was time to leave. I was bored. After 14 years as chief, the challenges were gone; there wasn't anything I hadn't done ... I had stayed as long as I cared to. No one had run me out."

Daryl Gates went on to subsequent careers as a radio talk show host and a videogame designer.

STALIN WORLD

THE OFFICIAL CITATION
THE IG NOBEL PEACE PRIZE WAS AWARDED TO

Viliumas Malinauskas of Grutas, Lithuania, for creating the amusement park known as "Stalin World."

The Grutas Sculpture Park, better known as "Stalin World," is at Grutas, 4690 Druskininkai, Lithuania. Telephone: (370 233) 55484, 52507, 52246, 47709; Fax: (370 233) 47451.

Viliumas Malinauskas is a man of immense strength, imagination, and mordant humor. Long ago, he was heavyweight wrestling champion of Lithuania. He served, not exactly by choice, in the Soviet Army, and later managed a collective farm. After the communist system collapsed, Mr. Malinauskas created an international mushroom distribution business, which made him wealthy. But he was somewhat bored until 1998, the year a collection of Soviet statues went up for auction. These were not just any statues. These were gigantic granite and bronze Lenins, Stalins, and other Official Soviet Heroes. Mr. Malinauskas realized that a man with money and wit, and a lack of affection for the old Soviet Union, might do something interesting with them.

They say of Stalin World that it "combines the charms of a Disneyland with the worst of the Soviet Gulag prison camp." Viliumas Malinauskas, on the whole, rather agrees. The neighbors are of varying opinions.

A promotional flyer from the Grutas Sculpture Park, which is popularly known—for good reason—as "Stalin World."

Stalin World is the only place in the neighborhood that's surrounded by barbed wire, and guard towers, and loudspeakers blaring Soviet-era military music.

A few people kicked at the idea of Stalin World, and tried to throw up roadblocks to its construction. Mr. Malinauskas at that point was 58 years old, tougher than nails, and had spent most of his life taking on Soviet apparatchiks. These nosy antiparkers stood no chance against him.

When Stalin World opened on April Fools' Day, 2001, Mr. Malinauskas honored the most vocal of these gadflies by putting up wooden statues of them near the front entrance. "Talking to them is just like talking to these," Mr. Malinauskas told a reporter from the *Sydney Morning Herald*, knocking the head of one of the wooden statues. "They have decided I'm wrong, but I say let the public be the judge."

Viliumas Malinauskas accepts the Ig Nobel Peace Prize, aided by the interpreter he brought with him from Lithuania to the ceremony at Harvard University. Four Nobel Laureates and numerous other dignitaries saluted Malinauskas by donning Stalin masks. Photo: Caroline Coffman/*Annals of Improbable Research*.

To build the park itself, Mr. Malinauskas drained a swamp, and installed more than a mile of winding, wooden walkways. The ambiance is pleasant, with pine, birch, and fir trees, a children's play area with seesaws and swings, and a small petting zoo with exotic birds. There's a cozy little café, information aplenty, and a place to buy souvenirs.

But the statues are the main attraction. There are more than 60 of them—Stalin, Lenin, and the other old favorites, larger and even harder than life. Some are missing body pieces—a head gone here, a hand or thumb there. But that just adds to the charm.

For visitors of a certain sensibility, the park's highlight is a replica of a 1941 railway station where guards in Soviet uniforms direct them onto cattle cars, which shuttle to a reconstruction of a prison camp. This is not for everyone.

On opening day, actors dressed as Lenin and Stalin handed out shots of vodka and tin bowls of borscht. Mr. Malinauskas wants the experience to be on the whole fun, and for those who are so inclined, also educational.

At the park's entrance, big red signs proclaim, "Happy New Year, Comrades!" The guides conduct tours in Lithuanian, Russian, or English. Overall, visitors find the experience to be much more pleasant than a place called Stalin World has any right to be.

For conceiving of Stalin World and making it a reality, Viliumas Malinauskas won the 2001 Ig Nobel Peace Prize.

Mr. Malinauskas, accompanied by his wife and an interpreter, travelled at his own expense from Grutas, Lithuania, to the Ig Nobel Prize Ceremony at Harvard. In accepting the Prize, this is what Mr. Malinauskas's interpreter said he said:

"Mr. Malinauskas wants to begin his speech with sincere greetings from a small carnival world that is situated near the Baltic Sea from Lithuania. He was invited here to tell you about the Grutas Park, which is popularly known here as Stalin World. According to such a given name, he would like to make you a present of a bronze bas-relief of Stalin.

"At the end of his speech, he would like to remind this honorable audience one very known old truth. It's better to see something once than to hear about it ten times, isn't it? So, dear ladies and gentlemen, he invites all of you to visit the wonderful country of Lithuania and as well to see the Grutas Park."

PEACEFUL EJACULATIONS AND EXPLOSIONS

 Some peacemakers favor an explosive approach to the process. Here are three exemplars:

- Booming Voices of Britain
- Father of the Bomb
- Pacific Kaboom

BOOMING VOICES OF BRITAIN

THE OFFICIAL CITATION
THE IG NOBEL PEACE PRIZE WAS AWARDED TO
The British Royal Navy, for ordering its sailors to stop using live cannon shells, and instead just to shout "Bang!"

The British Royal Navy found a way to save money and also bring a measure of peace and quiet. The method, albeit more traditional than some people realized, was hailed as an innovative, and perhaps portentous, way to ring in the year 2000.

The story, in a nutshell, was told in the May 20, 2000, issue of the *Guardian*:

"The Royal Navy has barred trainees at its top gunnery school from firing live shells and ordered them to shout 'bang' in a cost-cutting exercise. Sailors at the Gunnery and Naval Military Training School on land-based HMS *Cambridge*, near Plymouth, Devon, have been told to cry out into a microphone rather than pull the trigger after they have loaded shells and aimed their guns. They have previously fired live rounds from land-based turrets. It is believed that the move to cut back on shells, which cost £642 each, could save the Ministry of Defence £5 million over three years.

"One sailor said: 'You sit in a gun and shout "Bang, bang." You don't fire any ammunition. It's a big joke and the sailors are disgusted.' The sailor, serving on a warship, added: 'Junior ratings are coming aboard and they cannot fire guns without specialists watching them. It is causing dismay. You used to hear the sound of gunfire coming from HMS *Cambridge*—now all there is are shouts of "Bang, bang" over the microphone.'"

The imperative to say "bang" is in fact an honored tradition in the British armed forces. In his book *Adolf Hitler: My Part in His Downfall*, military historian Spike Milligan documents an instance of Just-Say-"Bang"ism in which he took part during World War II:

"There was one drawback. No ammunition. This didn't deter [our sergeant-major], he soon had all the gun crews shouting 'Bang' in unison. 'Helps keep morale up,' he told visiting [General] Alanbrooke. By luck, a 9.2 shell was discovered in Woolwich Rotunda. An official application was made: in due course the shell arrived. A guard was mounted over it. The Mayor was invited to inspect it, the Mayoress was photographed alongside it with a V for Victory sign: I don't think she had the vaguest idea what it meant. A month later, application was made to HQ Southern Command to fire the shell. The date was set for July 2, 1940. The day prior, we went round Bexhill carrying placards: 'THE NOISE YOU WILL HEAR TOMORROW AT MIDDAY WILL BE THAT OF BEXHILL'S OWN CANNON. DO NOT BE AFRAID.'"

Milligan further reports that the shell turned out to be a dud.

That was the army, and that was 1940. The navy has always tried to be more methodical than its sister service, and thus sometimes works more slowly. It took them a full 60 years to adopt the new innovation, but adopt it they did.

For bravely taking firm, quiet action, the British Royal Navy won the Ig Nobel Peace Prize in the year 2000.

The winners could not, or would not, attend the Ig Nobel Prize Ceremony. Instead, Richard Roberts, a 1993 Nobel Laureate in Physiology or Medicine and himself a native of England, accepted temporary custody of the Prize. (See page 66.) Roberts also vowed to spend the next year, if necessary, seeking someone in the navy to whom he could hand over the Prize. He did spend the year trying, but he did not succeed. Dr. Roberts still has custody of the Prize, and it is hoped that some high official of the navy will get in touch with him to arrange for delivery to a proper permanent place of enshrinement.

In the weeks following the Ceremony, the Ig Nobel Board of

Nobel Laureate Richard Roberts accepts temporary custody of the Ig Nobel Prize on behalf of the winners. Photo: Andrea Kulosh/*Annals of Improbable Research*.

Governors received letters from angry citizens of other nations, especially Germany, pointing out that their own militaries also Just Said "Bang," and so deserved a share of the Royal Navy's Ig Nobel Prize.

FATHER OF THE BOMB

THE OFFICIAL CITATION
THE IG NOBEL PEACE PRIZE WAS AWARDED TO
Edward Teller, father of the hydrogen bomb and first champion of the Star Wars weapons system, for his lifelong efforts to change the meaning of peace as we know it.

Edward Teller was one of the great scientists of the 20th century. Brilliant, gregarious, and blessed with the knowledge that he was always right, Teller also yearned to be one of the most influential scientists on world affairs. In personality and results, he was explosive.

Edward Teller is, in a sense, Mr. Bomb. He was part of almost every technical and political step in the history of the first atomic bomb and its progeny. He helped persuade the US government to build that first one, and took part in the now-famous Manhattan Project at Los Alamos, New Mexico, which did the actual building. History books say he spent most of his three years at Los Alamos nagging people and dreaming about the future. His fondest dream was to plan a new, even more powerful, kind of bomb.

The first atomic bomb was based on nuclear fission—splitting atoms apart to release a huge amount of energy in an explosion. Teller wanted a bomb that would squeeze atoms so much they would fuse together, releasing far, far more energy in a much, much bigger explosion. This new device would be called a "thermonuclear bomb."

Teller was still fond of the old-fashioned atomic bomb—but now he would use it in a supporting role. Just as it takes a little detonator cap to trigger off an old, old-fashioned chemical bomb, it takes a little atomic bomb to trigger off a thermonuclear bomb.

He pushed extremely hard to persuade the US government and the military to let him build a thermonuclear bomb. He got his way, though others did much of the technical work.

Many of the scientists who had built the earlier bomb urged caution. They took seriously a warning Teller himself gave them the first time he explained his plan. The thermonuclear bomb might generate enough heat to ignite the gases in the atmosphere or the oceans, effectively burning the earth's surface to a crisp. Teller didn't see this as a huge problem. Nor was he worried about other worries: the possible long-term radiation effects on bystanders; the possibility that building a new kind of weapon would cause other countries to bend heaven and earth to build one, too; the astronomical and endless cost of continuing to do this particular kind of technical work, and of the arms race.

The new bomb got built and tested. The atmosphere did not ignite, nor did the oceans. The Soviet Union did race to catch up and build their own thermonuclear bomb, and they succeeded. The cost of developing, building, and maintaining the bombs did rise even higher than anyone had foreseen, and much of the world was frightened to death.

Edward Teller was delighted. He continued to push for new kinds of weapons, the more technically difficult and expensive the better. He turned his wonderful imagination to new kinds of missile systems for sending bombs to far-off places. He noted that the Soviets tried to match everything he and his admirers came up with, so he vowed to always stay a few steps ahead, no matter what the cost, and no matter whether it was possible to get the thing to work.

As the decades rolled on, many of the new weapons did not, in fact, work, but Teller was relentlessly inventive and even more relentlessly demanding. If he could conceive of a weapon, then so might an enemy, and that was good reason to spend money on it. If he could conceive of a weapon to use against other weapons that he'd conceived of, even better.

Most historians believe that the so-called Star Wars missile defense plan of the 1980s got taken seriously, and got lavishly funded, because Edward Teller pushed so hard for it. The plan itself reportedly popped out of the fertile technical mind of US President Ronald Reagan, who thought it would be a splendid idea, though he himself didn't know what the idea was.

That and the other Teller-backed projects all have exciting names—X-ray laser weapons, "Brilliant Pebbles" kinetic-energy space-based interceptors, "pop-up deployment," "Super Excalibur," the "High Frontier" initiative. The list is long, and the investment in them is endless. These weapons by themselves are not enough to prevent the people of the earth from blowing each other up, Teller cautions, but they are necessary first steps in building enough weapons to do the job.

For supplying the world with such bursts of enthusiasm, Edward Teller won the 1991 Ig Nobel Peace Prize.

The winner could not, or would not, attend the Ig Nobel Prize Ceremony.

PACIFIC KABOOM

THE OFFICIAL CITATION
THE IG NOBEL PEACE PRIZE WAS AWARDED TO

Jacques Chirac, president of France, for commemorating the 50th anniversary of Hiroshima with atomic bomb tests in the Pacific.

Right after he took office, Jacques Chirac ordered up a fireworks display that would make everyone respect the power and glory of France.

On May 17, 1995, Chirac was sworn in as president of France. On June 13, he announced that his country would set off a string of thermonuclear bombs—on the other side of the world—triumphantly ending its three-year moratorium on testing nuclear weapons.

They would need a bit of quiet time to prepare, he said, but other than that delay, nothing would stop the show.

On July 16, he quietly celebrated the 50th anniversary of the first atomic explosion at Alamogordo, New Mexico.

On August 6, he quietly celebrated the 50th anniversary of the dropping of an atomic bomb on Hiroshima.

On August 9, he quietly celebrated the 50th anniversary of the dropping of an atomic bomb on Nagasaki.

On August 10, President Chirac announced the capstone of his plans. France would spend an entire year or so performing its series of wonderful nuclear fireworks exhibitions. Then, after their final performance, they would retire from the business, and support an international comprehensive test ban treaty so that no one ever again would set off "any nuclear weapon test explosion or any other nuclear explosion."

On August 17, an annoying distraction came from the competition. China, the only nuclear power that hadn't stopped setting off test explosions, set off another of its homemade bombs at its Lop Nor test site. In France, some thought this a very strange thing—a country exploding a nuclear bomb on its own territory.

September 5 was Jacques Chirac's big day. France set off a 20-kiloton thermonuclear explosion at the Moruroa Atoll in the South Pacific.

New Zealand and Australia, which are much closer to what was left of Moruroa than France is, got angry and complained. President Chirac said they were being "demagogic." New Zealand even asked the International Court of Justice in The Hague to tell France to call off its other scheduled performances. On September 22, the court rejected New Zealand's request.

On October 1, France set off a 110-kiloton thermonuclear bomb at the Fangataufa Atoll, which was not far from Moruroa.

On October 6, Jacques Chirac won the 1995 Ig Nobel Peace Prize. The winner could not, or would not, attend the Ig Nobel Prize Ceremony.

He celebrated by having France set off a 60-kiloton thermonuclear bomb on October 27, back at Moruroa Atoll, then set off further thermonuclear fireworks displays at the same place on November 21 (40 kilotons) and December 27 (30 kilotons).

After a pause to celebrate New Year's, they staged a 120-kiloton fireworks display on January 27, at Fangataufa. Two days later, Jacques Chirac called an early end to the exhibitions. The massive international protests had nothing to do with the early ending, President Chirac said. "I know that the decision that I made last June may have provoked, in France and abroad, anxiety and emotion. I know that nuclear weaponry may cause fear. But, in an always dangerous world, it acts for us as a weapon in the service of peace."

LOVE AND/OR REPRODUCTION

 Most human beings display considerable ingenuity in their attempts to produce new generations. Here are five Prize-winning cases of reproductive resourcefulness:

- The Compulsive Biochemistry of Love
- High-Velocity Birth
- Taking Fatherhood in Hand
- Insert Here
- Height, Penile Length, and Foot Size

THE COMPULSIVE
BIOCHEMISTRY OF LOVE

THE OFFICIAL CITATION
THE IG NOBEL CHEMISTRY PRIZE WAS AWARDED TO

Donatella Marazziti, Alessandra Rossi, and Giovanni B. Cassano of the University of Pisa, and Hagop S. Akiskal of the University of California (San Diego), for their discovery that, biochemically, romantic love may be indistinguishable from having severe obsessive-compulsive disorder.

Their study was published as "Alteration of the Platelet Serotonin Transporter in Romantic Love," *Psychological Medicine,* **vol. 29, no. 3, May 1999, pp. 741–5.**

Hundreds, perhaps thousands, of songs, poems, novels, and movies explore the link between obsession, compulsion, and romantic love. Donatella Marazziti, Alessandra Rossi, Giovanni B. Cassano, and Hagop S. Akiskal undertook the first thorough biochemical investigation of this complex and delicate question.

Doctors Marazziti, Rossi, Cassano, and Akiskal did things, as all good scientists do, systematically. They began by honorably declaring their interest: "Since falling in love is a natural phenomenon with obvious implications for the process of evolution, it is reasonable to hypothesize that it must be mediated by a well-established biological process." Next, they declared their intent: "In this report we examine the relationship between the serotonin (5-HT) transporter, the state of being in love and obsessive-compulsive processes."

The preliminaries being out of the way, they got down to business.

Before we get down to business, here is a quick word about technical matters: the chemical they mention—serotonin (5-HT), is involved in regulating all sorts of behavior, including appetite, sleep, arousal, and depression. It is the same chemical that caught the fancy of Professor Peter Fong of Gettysburg University, in Gettysburg, Pennsylvania, whose experiments with feeding Prozac to clams earned him an Ig Nobel Prize in 1998. (See the section of this book titled "The Happiness of Clams.")

Doctors Marazziti, Rossi, Cassano, and Akiskal simplified the entire romantic/obsessive/compulsive morass down to two simple questions:

1. Is romance literally in people's blood? And, if so,
2. Is it similar to what's in the blood of obsessive-compulsives?

They already knew that the two-headed monster of obsession and compulsion does, in a measurable sense, flow through the bloodstream. Other scientists had shown that people with obsessive-compulsive disorder have a very different amount of serotonin in their blood than do their nonobsessive, noncompulsive neighbors.

The investigation, then, would be straightforward. They would look at people who were suffering from obsessive-compulsive disorder, and also look at people who were suffering the transports of romantic love. They would compare the blood of both groups with the cooler, laid-back, more prosaic blood of steady, run-of-the-mill, not-in-love, nonobsessive, noncompulsive Janes and Joes.

They decided to examine 20 of each kind. It was easy to find 20 obsessive-compulsives, and also 20 dull people. The task of finding 20 people in love, though, was tricky, because there was no established scientific definition of "romantic love."

Of necessity, Drs. Marazziti, Rossi, Cassano, and Akiskal devised their own definition. This is how it appeared in their published report:

"20 subjects (17 female and three male, mean age: 24) who had recently fallen in love, were recruited from medical students, by means of advertisement. They were selected according to the following criteria:

1. the love relationship had begun within the previous six months;
2. the couple had had no sexual intercourse; and
3. at least four hours a day were spent thinking of the partner."

This definition later proved controversial (see below).

The blood tests gave results that Drs. Marazziti, Rossi, Cassano, and Akiskal found stunningly clear:

"The statistically significant decrease in the [blood levels] of subjects who were in love and in those of obsessive-compulsive disorder patients would seem to suggest a certain similarity between the two conditions . . . It would suggest that being in love literally induces a state which is not normal—as is indeed suggested by a variety of colloquial expressions used throughout the ages in different countries, all of which refer generally to falling 'insanely' in love or to being 'lovesick.'"

Dr. Marazziti and her colleagues also looked at what happened after the first blush of romance had dimmed. A year after the first blood tests, they interviewed the lovebirds and took new blood samples. Six were still in love with the same people, but no longer thought about their partners day and night. The blood of these six people had become similar to the dull blood of old married couples. Once again, science seemed to confirm what the poets of antiquity knew so well.

For exploring the chemistry of romance and the romance of chemistry, Donatella Marazziti, Alessandra Rossi, Giovanni B. Cassano and Hagop S. Akiskal won the 2000 Ig Nobel Prize in the field of Chemistry.

Donatella Marazziti planned to attend the Ig Nobel Prize Ceremony at her own expense. However, her husband fell ill, and Dr. Marazziti sent her acceptance speech via audiotape. In it, she said:

"Research on love is very important, because love is the engine of human life and of the universe. However, I'm sure that despite all of our efforts, the secrets of nature will remain elusive. I only provide this small insight into the biological mechanism of this typically human feeling. The main bias of my research was that the sample was constituted mainly of Italians, and the Italian way of falling in love may be quite different than that of other populations, such as the Americans. I regret not to be with you, and I send you my best regards and wishes for a joyful ceremony. Please continue to enjoy life, and continue to fall in love."

HIGH-VELOCITY BIRTH

THE OFFICIAL CITATION
THE IG NOBEL MANAGED HEALTH-CARE PRIZE WAS AWARDED TO

The late George and Charlotte Blonsky of New York City and San Jose, California, for inventing a device (US Patent #3,216,423) to aid women in giving birth; the woman is strapped onto a circular table, and the table is then rotated at high speed.

Childbirth can be slow and distressing. Inspired by elephants, a childless New York City couple designed a massive electromechanical device that considerably speeds up the process.

George Blonsky was a trained engineer—a mining engineer, as it happened—with an unusually cultivated taste for adventure and invention. Before moving to New York City, he and his wife, Charlotte, had owned and operated gold and tungsten mines in several parts of the world. George was forever inventing things, though not all of his creations made it past the blueprint stage. George and Charlotte loved children, though they had none, and had written several children's books, none of which were ever published.

They also loved the Bronx Zoo. One day George happened upon the sight of a pregnant elephant slowly twirling herself in circles, evidently in preparation for delivering a 250-pound baby.

The anatomical physics of it galvanized George Blonsky. George performed a simple technical analysis, and discerned the basic principles at work. He then wondered, as engineers will, whether his new-gained technological insight could somehow benefit humanity. Yes, it could, he decided. Yes, it could.

Thus was born the idea of the Blonsky device.

In their patent application, George and Charlotte explained the need for their invention:

"In the case of a woman who has a fully-developed muscular system and has had ample physical exertion all through the pregnancy, as is common with all more primitive peoples, nature provides all the necessary equipment and power to have a normal and quick delivery. This is not the case, however, with more civilized women who often do not have the opportunity to develop the muscles needed in confinement."

And, therefore, George and Charlotte wrote, they would provide "an apparatus which will assist the under-equipped woman by creating a gentle, evenly distributed, properly directed, precision-controlled force, that acts in unison with and supplements her own efforts."

The heart of the idea they expressed in a mere nine words: "The fetus needs the application of considerable propelling force."

George and Charlotte knew how to supply that propelling force.

The rest of their patent—eight very detailed pages altogether—specified exactly how to do it. The design includes some 125 basic components, including bolts, brakes, wing nuts, a massive concrete floor slab, a vari-speed vertical gear motor, a speed reducer, more wing nuts, sheaves, stretchers, shafts, thigh members, a butt plate, aluminum ballast water boxes, still more wing nuts, pillow clamps, a girdle member, and some additional wing nuts.

The patent specifies, in words and diagrams, how the parts are to be combined. Each is numbered for clarity. For example:

"The body of the mother is firmly held in position against movement as a whole under such forces by the boot members (73), the thigh holders (68), the girdle (61), the hand grips (79), and the belts (82), (83) and (84)."

The Blonskys sent the completed patent application off to Washington. On November 9, 1965, the US Patent Office granted them the patent for what would henceforth be officially called an "Apparatus

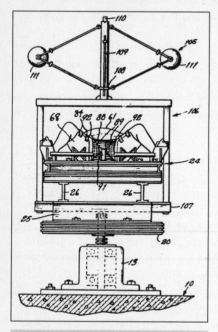

A side view of the Blonsky device. Note the small net for catching the child as it emerges. Some engineers feel it may be inadequate to the task, thus constituting a weak point in an otherwise admirable design.

for Facilitating the Birth of a Child by Centrifugal Force."

For conceiving what appears to be the greatest labor-saving device ever invented, George and Charlotte Blonsky won the 1999 Ig Nobel Prize in the field of Managed Health Care.

George Blonsky died in 1985, and Charlotte passed away in 1998, just a year before the Ig Nobel Board of Governors honored their achievement.

The Blonskys' niece, Gale Sturtevant, flew 3,000 miles from northern California to the ceremony at Harvard, at her own expense, to accept the Prize in honor of her aunt and uncle. Sturtevant said she has all of George and Charlotte's remaining papers, along with models of various inventions, stored unexamined in her garage. So far as she knows, George and Charlotte never built a full-scale centrifugal birthing device.

"In theory, you know, the idea might work," she told a newspaper reporter. "Uncle George was undoubtedly the most intelligent person I have ever met," added her husband, Don. "His mind was always active."

Several days after the Ig Nobel Ceremony, Dr. Andrea Dunaif, director of the Harvard Medical School's Center for Excellence in Women's Health, gave a lecture at the medical school about the Blonsky device. While expressing certain reservations about technical aspects of the apparatus, Dr. Dunaif concluded that the Blonskys "were well intentioned."

In subsequent months, the Ig Nobel Board of Governors heard from several women in the final stages of pregnancy. All delivered much the same message. "I know most people think that machine is funny, and so do I," said one, "but after nine months I'm really bored and tired of waiting for this birth. If that machine were available, I'd use it."

The
Ig Nobel
Prizes

SAFETY FIRST

The Blonskys carefully designed their device to ensure the safety of both mother and child. The machinery includes something known as a "speed governor," which ensures that neither mother nor child can be subjected to a dangerously strong level of force. When operating at its maximum spin rate, the machine would produce a force of seven Gs—seven times the normal force of gravity. (Note: pilots of jet fighter aircraft typically black out at a force of around five Gs.)

TAKING FATHERHOOD IN HAND

THE OFFICIAL CITATION

THE IG NOBEL BIOLOGY PRIZE WAS AWARDED TO

Dr. Cecil Jacobson, relentlessly generous sperm donor, and prolific patriarch of sperm banking, for devising a simple, single-handed method of quality control.

The book *The Babymaker: Fertility Fraud and the Fall of Dr. Cecil Jacobson*, by Rick Nelson, Bantam Books, 1994, tells much of the story of Dr. Jacobson and his adventures.

Dr. Cecil Jacobson was a family man in oh, so many ways, some pleasing, some perhaps otherwise. On the one hand, there were the babies that never existed—Dr. Jacobson told hundreds of women they were pregnant when, in fact, they were not. On the other hand, although Dr. Jacobson never mentioned it to his patients who did have babies, he was the biological father of a remarkable number of their children. Doctor Jacobson's own wife claimed to be pleased and proud about this.

Dr. Cecil Jacobson ran a fertility clinic in Vienna, Virginia, a prosperous suburb of Washington, DC. He specialized in helping women get pregnant.

The clinic consisted of Dr. Jacobson as the only physician, and a varying staff of drudge workers including his wife, Joyce, some of their own large brood of children, and, until the money ran short, a very small number of other administrative workers.

Customers flocked to the clinic. Dr. Jacobson had a considerable reputation, based on some very real early accomplishments followed by years of loud, quasi-accurate boasting. When a young man, Dr. Jacobson was among the pioneers in using amniocentesis to diagnose the health of a developing fetus. After that, though, he moved from job to job, from hospital to hospital, as one boss after another decided that the celebrated Dr. Jacobson was ever more a creature of words than of genuine accomplishments. After being quietly but forcefully terminated from these places of employ, he would falsely claim to be still affiliated with them.

Couples who have difficulty conceiving a child sometimes grow desperate. In the Washington area, Dr. Jacobson was the one to whom the most anxious, the apparently hopeless cases would be referred.

Unlike other doctors who deal with pregnancy and childbirth, Dr. Jacobson seldom gave his new patients any kind of examination. Nor, typically, did he ask many questions. What he did was talk.

Dr. Jacobson was a real talker. He'd tell a woman he was going to get her pregnant. Sometimes he would guarantee it. He'd instruct her to have sex with her husband diligently and often. He insisted that some couples have sex every day for weeks on end.

The genius lay in what else he did. He would inject the woman with a generally innocuous hormone called human chorionic gonadotrophin (HCG). This accomplished two good things for Dr. Jacobson. First, it brought in lots of money, because he charged for every injection and he would give patients dozens and dozens of them. Dr. Jacobson bought so much HCG that his tiny one-doctor clinic was reportedly one of the largest purchasers of HCG in the world; he bought at very low cost and then marked up the price tremendously.

The HCG injections also brought delight, albeit temporarily, to the patients. All that HCG in their bloodstreams caused the women to register positive on a simple pregnancy test. In at least one case, Dr. Jacobson told a 49-year-old postmenopausal woman that she would get pregnant, then he injected her with lots of HCG, and voilà, a pregnancy test indicated she was with child.

After announcing the "good news," Dr. Jacobson would use ul-trasonography to produce a fuzzy—extremely fuzzy—"picture" of what he said was a fetus. This sent the supposedly imminent parents into giddy rapture. He would then take new sonograms over the succeeding weeks and months, each time producing an indecipher-ably fuzzed sonogram image that supposedly showed a developing fetus.

Dr. Jacobson would warn the supposedly pregnant women not to go see their regular obstetricians, saying it would somehow endanger the pregnancy. Patients who, despite the warning, did go see their own doctors got a jarring surprise: they were not pregnant. When a distressed woman would then ask Dr. Jacobson how this could be, he explained that the pregnancy had spontaneously aborted, and that the fetus had been completely "absorbed" into the mother's body, leaving no trace. He would then recommend a new round of HCG in-jections and regular sexual intercourse. Many of his patients followed that advice, repeatedly, enduring years of heartbreak.

All that would have been enough to earn Cecil Jacobson a place in history. It was enough to get the press and the police interested. But Dr. Jacobson's greatest fame came from an additional little ser-vice he provided to some of his patients.

Some women did conceive while under Dr. Jacobson's care. These women he did immediately send back to their own obstetricians to oversee the pregnancy. Some of these pregnancies were the result of nature taking its course, others started with artificial insemination that had been recommended and performed by Cecil Jacobson.

Dr. Jacobson told each of the artificial insemination patients that he used anonymous sperm donors, whose physical characteristics he matched to those of the woman's husband. In fact, Dr. Jacobson himself donated all of the sperm.

In 1991, Cecil Jacobson was brought up on 53 counts of fraud. Prosecutors made it clear that they were presenting just the tip of the iceberg. They estimated that Dr. Jacobson's sperm, hand delivered by Dr. Jacobson, had produced as many as 75 children. To the end, a small band of supporters, including US Senator Orrin Hatch from Cecil Jacobson's native state of Utah, maintained that the doctor was

a saintly, heroic man who had been unfairly maligned and perse-
cuted. Dr. Jacobson was convicted on all counts, and got a prison
sentence. He also got the 1992 Ig Nobel Prize in the field of Biology.
The winner could not, or would not, attend the Ig Nobel Prize Ceremony. He had a previous five-year engagement.

THE OFFICIAL CITATION
THE IG NOBEL MEDICINE PRIZE WAS AWARDED TO

Willibrord Weijmar Schultz, Pek van Andel, and Eduard Mooyaart of Groningen, the Netherlands, and Ida Sabelis of Amsterdam, for their illuminating report, "Magnetic Resonance Imaging of Male and Female Genitals During Coitus and Female Sexual Arousal."

Their study was published in the *British Medical Journal*, vol. 319, 1999, pp. 1596–1600. The full version of Ida Sabelis's first-hand account of her experience was published in the *Annals of Improbable Research*, vol. 7, no. 1, January/February 2001, pp. 13–14.

A research team in the Netherlands gave humanity its first good, inside look at a couple's genitals while those genitals were in use.

It is possible to fit two people inside the cylinder of a magnetic resonance imaging machine, and this in turn makes it possible to take MRI images of the couple's sex organs in operation, if the two people are not claustrophobic.

The research team recruited several couples who were willing and able to perform under these technologically cloistered conditions, and who had all the requisite equipment, including, in the case of the females, an intact uterus and ovaries. The scientists assured the participants that there would be confidentiality, privacy, and anonymity. (After the couples had donned their clothing, though, some of them happily chose to shed their anonymity.)

The setup had a distinctly clinical feel: "The tube in which the couple would have intercourse stood in a room next to a control room where the researchers were sitting behind the scanning console and screen. An improvised curtain covered the window between the two rooms, so the intercom was the only means of communication."

The arrangement was in some ways not unlike those of early NASA astronauts in their space capsules, exchanging instructions and acknowledgments by radio link. In other ways, the arrangement was unlike those of early NASA astronauts in their space capsules.

The experimental procedure was straightforward:

"The first image was taken with [the woman] lying on her back. Then the male was asked to climb into the tube and begin face-to-face coitus in the superior position. After this shot—successful or not—the man was asked to leave the tube and the woman was asked to stimulate her clitoris manually and to inform the researchers by intercom when she had reached the preorgasmic stage. Then she stopped the autostimulation for a third image. After that image was taken, the woman restarted the stimulation to achieve an orgasm. Twenty minutes after the orgasm, the fourth image was taken."

That's all there was to it.

Six of the couples succeeded in at least partial penetration. Two couples were invited to repeat the procedure one hour after the man had taken Viagra. Both couples accepted the offer, with positive results.

The overall results were impressive. As the researchers described them in their published report:

"The images obtained showed that during intercourse in the 'missionary position' the penis has the shape of a boomerang and $1/3$ of its length consists of the root of the penis. During female sexual arousal without intercourse, the uterus was raised and the anterior vaginal wall lengthened. The size of the uterus did not increase during sexual arousal."

The scientists were quietly triumphant, because their objectives were largely met. They *did* find out whether taking images of the male and female genitals during coitus is feasible, and they *did*, to some limited extent, find out whether former and current ideas

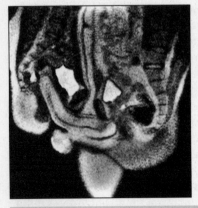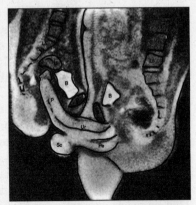

An original image published in the *British Medical Journal* from the MRI session, and a copy in which the investigators have helpfully outlined the areas of special interest.

about the anatomy during sexual intercourse and during female sexual arousal are based on assumptions or on facts.

For their contributions to the study of anatomy and physiology, Willibrord Weijmar Schultz, Pek van Andel, Eduard Mooyaart, and Ida Sabelis won the 2000 Ig Nobel Prize in the field of Medicine.

Pek van Andel traveled, at his own expense, from Groningen, the Netherlands, to the Ig Nobel Prize Ceremony. In accepting the Prize, he said:

"To find something truly new you need an unpredictable element: a strange observation, idea or experiment. The new comes—by definition—by surprise. When I saw an odd scan of the throat of a singer, singing an 'Aaa . . . ,' I wondered: Why not a scan of a love act?

"The hardware was no problem. Removing the table from the scanner tube gave enough space to make love. The software? No problem, we programmed the machine to do a scan of a 'patient' of '300 pounds.' The wetware? We had enough slim volunteers. The only problem was the Red Tape, so we had to do our work clandestinely.

"Our first scans revealed an amazing anatomy. A penis as a

boomerang with a huge root. An unchanged uterus and a fast-filling urine bladder!

"Three times our article was refused for publication. Twice by *Nature* magazine and once by the *British Medical Journal*. Finally the *British Medical Journal* took it, after a check in Holland, behind our back, as to whether the article was fake or not. The lesson of this is you should cherish your idiot idea, and push it through—even through your boss or bosses, if need be."

The day after the Ig Nobel Ceremony, Dr. van Andel lectured at Harvard Medical School, giving technical information and advice for those who would like to undertake this line of research. The audience of doctors was hushed and amazed.

HEIGHT, PENILE LENGTH, AND FOOT SIZE

THE OFFICIAL CITATION

THE IG NOBEL STATISTICS PRIZE WAS AWARDED TO

Jerald Bain of Mt. Sinai Hospital in Toronto, and Kerry Siminoski of the University of Alberta, for their carefully measured report, "The Relationship Among Height, Penile Length, and Foot Size."

Their study was published in the *Annals of Sex Research*, vol. 6, no. 3, 1993, pp. 231–5.

Science at its best determines whether what "everyone" believes is in fact true. Dr. Jerald Bain and Dr. Kerry Siminoski examined one of mankind's cherished and feared beliefs. They attacked this problem with a ruler.

"One of the more prevalent beliefs," wrote Dr. Bain and Dr. Siminoski, "involves the theory that the size of a man's penis may be estimated indirectly by assessing overall body size, or by gauging the size of another of his appendages (such as his ear lobes, nose, thumbs, or feet), and extrapolating to penile length. Depending on the underlying hypothesis, the penis is assumed to correlate either directly or inversely with the dimensions of one of these other body parts. To scientifically address this, we studied the relationships among penis length and two of these anatomic variables, overall body height and foot length."

To do this, Dr. Bain and Dr. Siminoski recruited 63 men who were willing to have their pertinent body parts measured. In their report,

Dr. Bain and Dr. Siminoski do not specify what method they used to recruit the men.

Dr. Bain and Dr. Siminoski measured the body parts. The heights ranged from 157 to 194 centimeters. The feet ranged from 24.4 to 29.4 centimeters. The penises ranged from 6.0 to 13.5 centimeters. Penis length was measured while the penises were stretched. In their report, Dr. Bain and Dr. Siminoski do not specify what method they used to stretch the penises.

With the data in hand, Dr. Bain and Dr. Siminoski did a statistical analysis. Dr. Bain and Dr. Siminoski specify that the method they used was a least-squares linear regression.

Their analysis indicated that there is what they call a "weak" correlation between a man's height and the length of his penis, and that there is also a "weak" correlation between his foot size and his penis length.

Their final conclusion: "Our data . . . indicate that there is no practical utility in predicting penis size from foot size or height."

For making statistics interesting to the common man, Dr. Jerald Bain and Dr. Kerry Siminoski won the 1998 Ig Nobel Prize in the field of Statistics.

Dr. Bain traveled, at his own expense, from Toronto to the Ig Nobel Prize Ceremony. In accepting the Prize, he said:

"This is a real study, and it's a very important study, and I hope you'll all take it seriously. There has been an old folk mythology about the relationship between certain bodily appendages and foot size. Now, I wasn't really aware of this mythology until some years ago when my late mother-in-law—my dear late mother-in-law—she was a wonderful woman—I loved her dearly, I think she loved me dearly . . .

"One day after we had three children—we now have four—my mother-in-law said to my wife, 'Did you see how small Jerry's feet are?' So Sheila, my dear wife, said, 'So?' And her response was, 'Don't you know?'

"This research was spurred on to answer the eternal question. I must tell you that the answer is that, yes, there is a very—and it's hard to find the right words when talking about this—there is a very weak relationship. But there is also a relationship between penile size and height, so that taller, bigger people—it's just a reflection of body size—but, take heart, take heart, because it would be foolish and frivolous of any woman to try to judge the potential size of the— it would be very difficult, because the most important fact to know is that the erection is the great equalizer."

The following day, Dr. Bain lectured at Harvard, explaining his fascination and expertise in penile and other body-part measurement, and illustrating his points with colorful slides, statistics, and personal memorabilia.

As Harvard physics professor Roy Glauber sweeps paper airplanes from the stage, Nobel Laureates (right to left) Richard Roberts, William Lipscomb, and Dudley Herschbach display their gigantic footwear. Sheldon Glashow (visible over Glauber's shoulder) rushes to join them. The Laureates took their stand as a tribute to Bain and Siminoski's Prize-winning report, "The Relationship Among Height, Penile Length, and Foot Size." Photo: Eric Workman/*Annals of Improbable Research.*

DISCOVERIES—
BASIC SCIENCE

Scientific breakthroughs are called "breakthroughs" because they are so surprising. They come against and break though a great wall of expectation. This chapter describes four very surprising discoveries that were eventually, and inevitably, honored by Ig Nobel Prizes:

- The Happiness of Clams
- Cold Fusion in Chickens
- Mini-Dinosaurs, Mini-Princesses
- The Remembrance of Water Passed

THE HAPPINESS
OF CLAMS

THE OFFICIAL CITATION
THE IG NOBEL BIOLOGY PRIZE WAS AWARDED TO
Peter Fong of Gettysburg College, Gettysburg, Pennsylvania, for contributing to the happiness of clams by giving them Prozac.

The study was published as "Induction and Potentiation of Parturition in Fingernail Clams (*Sphaerium striatinum*) by Selective Serotonin Re-Uptake Inhibitors (SSRIs)," Peter F. Fong, Peter T. Huminski, and Lynette M. D'urso, *Journal of Experimental Zoology*, vol. 280, 1998, pp. 260–4.

Ever since its introduction in 1987, Prozac has been one of the most prescribed antidepressant drugs. It is used to treat human beings, and sometimes also cats, dogs, and other pets.

Professor Peter Fong gave Prozac to clams, and he had a very good reason for doing so.

It's mostly about sex.

The drug fluoxetine—popularly known as Prozac—helps rouse many patients from a severe depression. That is the main reason for its sudden and great popularity with both doctors and patients. Like many medicines, fluoxetine's effects can be hit-or-miss: for some people it works like magic, for others, it does little or nothing. For some patients the effect is more like hit-and-run: in these people fluoxetine seems to lessen or kill the sexual drive.

But when it comes to sex, there have long been intriguing hints that fluoxetine can work in the opposite direction. A 1993 report in the *Journal of Clinical Psychiatry* concluded that the "Sexual side effects of fluoxetine may be more variable than previously thought." The report's title: "Association of Fluoxetine and Return of Sexual Potency in Three Elderly Men."

So it was perhaps not entirely out of the realm of possibility that when Prozac was fed to clams, it would have some happy effect on the little animals' sex lives. Knowing this possibility, though, did not fully prepare Peter Fong for the magnitude of the effect. When he fed fluoxetine to clams, the results were, in sexual terms, spectacular.

Fong fed the fluoxetine to clams as an experiment. He chose clams because clams and humans (and cows, lobsters, squid, and a multitude of other animals) show some remarkable similarities way deep down in their nervous systems. On the cellular level, much of what transpires in the clam is remarkably like what goes on in people. By studying the nervous system of clams—tinkering, measuring, feeding it Prozac—scientists can sometimes learn surprisingly useful amounts of information about human beings. Experiments on clams often, in addition, can be done more quickly, more cheaply, and with less paperwork than corresponding experiments on humans.

Fong's fluoxetine findings were not without scientific import. Then and now, nobody fully understands how fluoxetine and its chemical cousins work. The actions of the nervous system are complex and subtle, defying anyone who tries to tease out their secrets. Nevertheless, Professor Peter Fong of Gettysburg College, Gettysburg, Pennsylvania, did find some hidden nuggets.

He found that if you feed Prozac to clams (at least to clams of the species *Sphaerium striatinum*, also known as "fingernail clams"), they begin reproducing furiously—at about 10 times their normal rate.

Thus, thanks to Peter Fong, we know that Prozac has measurably profound effects on the nervous system and reproductive behavior of the fingernail clam. For demonstrating this, he won the 1998 Ig Nobel Prize in the field of Biology.

The winner could not attend the Ig Nobel Prize Ceremony, as he had to teach a class that day. Instead, he sent an acceptance speech to be presented at the ceremony. Here are Professor Fong's words, which were read aloud that evening by Dr. Peter Kramer, author of the book *Listening to Prozac*:

"Many people have asked me how I came upon using Prozac to make clams have sex. It happened quite by accident. It was late one night, and I was sitting alone in my laboratory feeling pretty depressed. Rising from my chair, I clumsily knocked over my prescription of Prozac and watched helplessly as several capsules fell into an aquarium full of clams. To my amazement, the clams began spawning copious amounts of sperm and eggs into the water. Suddenly, I was no longer depressed. The rest is history. I thank the manufacturers of Prozac, and I salute the clams—Nobel beasts who gave their lives for my research, but at least they had sex before they died and went out with a bang. Happy as a clam."

Professor Fong continued to do research on other aspects of reproductive biology and the ecology of aquatic invertebrates. In 2001, for example, he published a paper in the *Journal of Experimental Zoology* elucidating the mechanism of penile erection in the snail *Biomphalaria glabrata*.

Professor Fong has not wholly left behind the subject that earned him an Ig Nobel Prize. To the delight of those who savored his work with Prozac and clams, in 2002 he wrote a chapter for the book *Pharmaceuticals and Personal Care Products in the Environment* (published by the American Chemical Society Press). The chapter title: "Antidepressants in Aquatic Organisms."

COLD FUSION IN CHICKENS

THE OFFICIAL CITATION

THE IG NOBEL PHYSICS PRIZE WAS AWARDED TO

Louis Kervran of France, ardent admirer of alchemy, for his conclusion that the calcium in chickens' eggshells is created by a process of cold fusion.

His study was published as *A la Découverte des Transmutations Biologiques, Le Courrier des Livres, Paris, 1966.* It was translated into English, together with other of Kervran's scientific writings, and published as *Biological Transmutations and Their Applications in: Chemistry, Physics, Biology, Ecology, Medicine, Nutrition, Agronomy, Geology,* Swan House, 1972.

Chemistry is not as difficult as students fear. The equations taught in school are wrong. The so-called elements (hydrogen, helium, lithium, beryllium, boron, carbon, nitrogen, and all the rest) are not elemental at all. Transforming one into another—turning silicon into calcium, or manganese into iron—is easy. Happens all the time. Even a chicken can do it. In fact, chickens do do it.

This was Louis Kervran's message.

All of modern chemistry—which is to say all of chemistry since it became a science—is based on the idea that there are stable atoms of different kinds. An atom of iron is different from an atom of chlorine is different from an atom of silver is different from an atom of gold. Chemistry is all about how you stick lots of atoms together in bunches (the technical word is "compounds"), and how you recombine the bunches into other bunches. All the substances we encounter are formed by atoms bunching together this way and that.

All well and good, wrote Louis Kervran, but inside living creatures, "the improbable surely happens." Inside living creatures, atoms aren't limited to just palling around with other kinds of atoms. Inside living creatures, one kind of atom can turn into a different kind. An atom of silicon can become, voilà, an atom of calcium. An atom of iron can become an atom of manganese, or vice versa.

For centuries, optimists, cockeyed and otherwise, had hoped and prayed that base elements, such as lead, could be transmuted into expensive ones, such as gold. But no one had ever seen such things happening (except, in a very limited way, in the hellishly superheated confines of stars and nuclear explosions).

Scientists never noticed it happening, Louis Kervran explained, because they paid too much attention to dead solids and dead liquids and dead gases, when they should have been watching living flesh. "All laws of physics have been deduced from experiments made on dead matter," wrote Kervran.

Living tissue, he went on to explain, always carries out a process that he named "biological transmutation." The process is so simple, so basic, that Louis Kervran didn't bother to explain how or why it happens. It just happens. Biological transmutation can go in either of two directions:

- Sometimes two atoms of different kinds combine, forming a larger, third kind of atom. This is nuclear fusion. Years later other people coined a term that describes it well: "cold fusion."
- Other times a large atom will split into two smaller atoms, each of different kinds. This is nuclear fission.

The box overleaf ("A Guide: Transmuting One Element into Another") gives some technical details.

Physicists have never seen nuclear fusion or nuclear fission occur in living creatures. This, said Louis Kervran, is because they never looked. Louis Kervran looked, and here are just a few of the things he says he saw.

Chickens produce the calcium in their eggshells by transmuting potassium into calcium. A pig's intestines transmute nitrogen into carbon and oxygen. Cabbage transmutes oxygen into sulfur. Peaches transmute iron into copper.

In a report called "Non-Zero Balance of Calcium, Phosphorous and Copper in the Lobster," published in 1969, Kervran explained how lobsters perform nuclear fusion.

For his discovery of amazing things inside living flesh, Louis Kervran won the 1993 Ig Nobel Prize in the field of Physics.

The winner could not, or would not, attend the Ig Nobel Prize Ceremony.

The Ig Nobel Prizes

A GUIDE: TRANSMUTING ONE ELEMENT INTO ANOTHER

How exactly does biological transmutation work? It's apparently simple to see, and as Louis Kervran wrote: "There is no chemistry involved."

When you look at a periodic table of the elements, you see that every element has a so-called atomic number. The atomic number is the number of protons in the atom's nucleus. Here are a few elements, with their atomic numbers:

HYDROGEN—atomic number 1
SODIUM—atomic number 11
OXYGEN—atomic number 8
POTASSIUM—atomic number 19
CALCIUM—atomic number 20

The atomic numbers are the key to what is possible and what is not. Here are some examples, taken from Kervran's book, of how these elements transform, one kind becoming another.

(continued)

A GUIDE: TRANSMUTING ONE ELEMENT INTO ANOTHER
(*continued*)

• a **SODIUM** atom combines with an **OXYGEN** atom, and so becomes a **POTASSIUM** atom. [11 + 8 becomes 19]
• a **CALCIUM** atom splits into two pieces, a **HYDROGEN** atom and a **POTASSIUM** atom. [20 − 1 becomes 19]
• a **POTASSIUM** atom combines with a **HYDROGEN** atom, and so becomes a **CALCIUM** atom [19 + 1 becomes 20]

Kervran pointed out that "A law now emerges from these biological transformations: reactions at the nuclear level of the atom always involve hydrogen and oxygen."

He wrote that "it is usually vain to try to produce an element with biological transmutation if that element is not already present. In other words, what should be sought is the increase of an element (which always leads to the diminution of another), not its appearance from zero."

It should be noted that chemists and physicists all say they have never seen any of this happen, ever. Louis Kervran concluded that chemists and physicists are ignorant.

MINI-DINOSAURS, MINI-PRINCESSES

THE OFFICIAL CITATION
THE IG NOBEL BIODIVERSITY PRIZE WAS AWARDED TO

Chonosuke Okamura of the Okamura Fossil Laboratory in Nagoya, Japan, for discovering the fossils of dinosaurs, horses, dragons, princesses, and more than 1,000 other extinct "mini-species," each of which is less than $1/100$ of an inch in length.

His studies were published in the series *Original Report of the Okamura Fossil Laboratory,* published by the Okamura Fossil Laboratory in Nagoya, Japan, during the 1970s and 1980s.

Earle Spamer, a scientist based at the Academy of Natural Sciences, in Philadelphia, is the world's leading (and perhaps only) expert on Chonosuke Okamura. Spamer has written three articles attempting to explain Okamura's work. They were published in the *Annals of Improbable Research,* vol. 1, no. 4 (July/August 1995); vol. 2, no. 4, (July/August 1996); and vol. 6, no. 6 (November/December 2000). Much of the description below is adapted from Spamer's reports.

When a Japanese scientist examined rocks under a microscope, he discovered evidence that all modern living creatures are descended from tiny organisms resembling, in all but size, the big ones we see today. He gave a name to these extinct ancestor species: he called them "mini-creatures."

Chonosuke Okamura was a paleontologist who specialized in fossils of the unglamorous sort—invertebrate and algal specimens ranging in age from the Ordovician period to the Tertiary period. He published a series of dry, unglamorous reports.

But everything changed with the publication of *Original Report of the Okamura Fossil Laboratory*, number XIII. There Okamura showed photographs of a perfectly preserved fossil duck from the Silurian strata of the Kitagami mountain range—a previously unknown species he called *Archaeoanas japonica*. Okamura's illustration clearly shows the specimen just as he describes it: "in state of cramp through shock by being buried alive during the Silurian period." The specimen measures just 9.2 mm (0.36 inches) long. This mini-duck is about the size of an aspirin tablet.

Okamura's subsequent reports were filled with remarkable photographs of the fossilized remains of all sorts of mini-creatures, each documented in photographs, with helpful diagrams and riveting descriptions that Okamura wrote himself in a helpful mixture of Japanese and broken English.

He describes mini-fishes, mini-reptiles, mini-amphibians, mini-birds, mini-mammals, and mini-plants. There are even mini-dragons, such as *Fightingdraconus miniorientalis* and *Twistdraconus miniorientalis*.

Most of these newly discovered fossil taxa are subspecies of modern species. Okamora shows us the mini-lynx (*Lynx lynx minilorientalis*), the mini-gorilla (*Gorilla gorilla minilorientalis*), the mini-camel (*Camelus dromedarius minilorientalis*), the Silurian mini-snake (*Y. y. minilorientalis*), the mini-polar bear (*Thalarctos maritimus minilorientalus*), and the mini–common dog (*Canis familiaris minilorientalis*), whose "features were similar to those of a St. Bernard [sic] dog, but the length was only 0.5 mm."

Okamura also discovered the ancestral forms of extinct species; for example, a mini-pteradactyl (*Pteradactylus spectabilis minilorientalus*) and a children's perennial favorite, the mini-brontosaurus (*Brontosaurus excelsus minilorientalus*).

All of these creatures are less than a centimeter in length. Some are barely a millimeter long.

In most of the descriptions, Okamura combines scientific deduction with sympathetic observation. For example, in his description of *Lynx lynx minilorientalis* he notes:

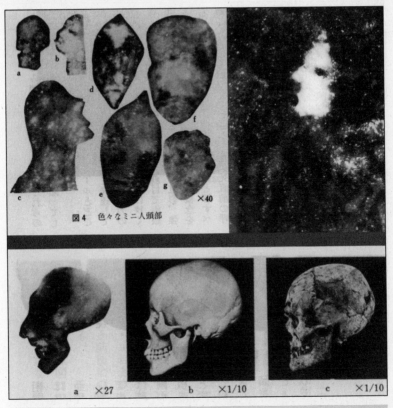

図4　色々なミニ人頭部

Fossils of mini-people, each of whom was approximately one millimeter tall. *Upper left*: Faces of mini-men. (Okamura cut these images from larger photographs, presumably to make them easier for nonspecialists to recognize.) *Upper right*: A specimen of *Homo sapiens minilorientalis*. Okamura wrote that she was a Nagaiwa mini-woman "about 30 years of age [and who] seems to be wearing a mantle of some kind on which many small dragons have been pasted, perhaps an after-death phenomenon." *Lower panel*: The skulls of a mini-man (left), a modern human (center) and an early hominid or proto-human (right). The mini-man skull is much smaller than the other two—an entire mini-man, from head to toe, was about as long as a modern infant's fingernail.

"Some look frightened in anger against a sudden convulsion of nature while others are indifferent or even have sunk their heads on their breasts having lost the power of resistance. These are remnant remained forms of psychical movement showing the degree of development of intelligence."

Certainly, Okamura's greatest claim to fame is the discovery of the mini-man, *Homo sapiens minilorientalis*. In a lengthy and meticulous anatomical discussion, illustrated with hundreds of photomicrographs, the earliest ancestors of humans are described. "The Nagaiwa mini-man had a stature of only 1/350 that of the Recent man but with the same shape." The tools of these mini-people are described, too, including "one of the first metallic implements."

Okamura gives us keen insights into the lives of these mini-people. Consider these three of his observations:

- "All the women in Figure 70 have closed mouths and [are] seen to be undergoing pain by being buried alive in boiling mud, while the old woman in Figure 1 has a wide open mouth, looking like one who has lost her senses."
- "In this photo, two totally-naked homos, facing each other, are moving their hands and feet harmoniously on good terms. We can think of no other scene than dancing in a present-day style."
- "They were polytheists and had many idols installed."

Okamura points out to us "the oldest hair styles"; "a quick-footed Nagaiwa mini-woman [who was] probably a hard worker"; a mini-woman who "seems to have been a person of noble rank"; and the "head of a mini-man in the alimentary canal of a dragon."

The Nagaiwa mini-people were artisans, too, producing a broad variety of sculpture. "What may be regarded as the most elaborate piece of work," Okamura tells us, is that of a "full-length portrait of a woman sitting on the neck of a dragon," who "may be putting on a hat." Okamura "presumes this to be some kind of goddess," whose "mammae seem to be quite swollen and sagging a little."

The Nagaiwa mini-world was not idyllic. Okamura illustrates a

"Close nestling protomini-man and protomini-woman . . . both defying a dragon"; a "dragon strangling a girl"; and a "mini-man offering a sacrifice to a brutal dragon"; among other insightful tableaux. However, this review cannot even begin to place in proper perspective the wealth of detail described in Okamura's reports.

The relationship between mini-men and dragons appears to have been uncomfortable, if Okamura's interpretions are correct:

"From what the author could determine, the mini-men lived in the ancient times having a high intellectual level with only flat nails for protecting themselves. Even if they grasped poles, using their free upper limbs, or used primitive metallic arms which seem to have existed, or hurled simply processed stones, it would have been most difficult to escape from the gluttoneous [sic] desire of countless flesh-eating hungry dragons."

The earlier forms of mini-people were without hands, but, Okamura tells us, "it would have made no difference if there had been a hand-to-hand fight with dragons, they still would have been defeated without the least resistance. The dragons would have mortally wounded them and crushed their bodies."

Okamura's startling observations were not totally devoid of emotion. He wrote, "The author will do his best to comfort their departed spirits."

The Okamura Fossil Laboratory has apparently not produced any new work since circa 1987. Chonosuke Okamura himself appears to have retired to a secluded life. His carefully detailed work simply drifted into obscurity, a sad example of what can happen when a scientist gets inadequate publicity.

For discovering tiny clues about our past, Chonosuke Okamura won the 1996 Ig Nobel Prize in the field of Biodiversity.

The winner could not, or would not, attend the Ig Nobel Prize Ceremony. The Ig Nobel Board of Governors tried, and failed, to find him.

To find out where you can see Okamura's photographs, visit: www.improbable.com/ig/ig-pastwinners.html

THE REMEMBRANCE
OF WATER PASSED

THE OFFICIAL CITATION
THE IG NOBEL CHEMISTRY PRIZE WAS
AWARDED—TWICE—TO

Jacques Benveniste, prolific proseletizer and dedicated correspondent of *Nature*, for his persistent discoveries that water,
H_2O, is an intelligent liquid, and for demonstrating to his satisfaction that water is able to remember events long after all trace of
those events has vanished; and that not only does water have
memory, but the information can be transmitted over telephone
lines and the Internet.

**Jacques Benveniste's original study was published in the journal *Nature*
in 1988 ("Human Basophil Degranulation Triggered by Very Dilute
Antiserum Against IgE," *Nature*, vol. 333, no. 6176, June 30, 1988,
pp. 816–18), but was later withdrawn at the insistence of the editors.
His telephonic study was published as "Transatlantic Transfer of
Digitized Antigen Signal by Telephone Link," J. Benveniste, P. Jurgens, W.
Hsueh and J. Aissa, *Journal of Allergy and Clinical Immunology*—"Program
and Abstracts of Papers to Be Presented During Scientific Sessions
AAAAI/AAI.CIS Joint Meeting," February 21–26, 1997.**

Jacques Benveniste is the only person who has two Ig Nobel Prizes.
He was honored for his discoveries—his memorable and repeated discoveries—that water (H_2O) has abilities that nobody had noticed.

In 1988, Benveniste, till that time a respected biologist at the highly
respected INSERM (Institut National de la Santé et de la Recherche
Médicale) in Paris, published a research paper in the respected jour-

nal *Nature*. In high-grade, professionally obtuse technical language, the paper said (a) that water remembers things and (b) that Jacques Benveniste had proved it.

What's more, Benveniste told anyone who asked, his discovery explained how homeopathic medicines work.

Homeopathic drugs are, in effect, drugs that have had all the drug removed. Most scientists believe they don't work at all, except to the extent that people want to *believe* they work. After all, most good doctors and good scientists say bluntly, it's always been true that, for the most part, medicine consists of entertaining the patient whilst nature effects a cure.

Benveniste has been conducting his experiments for decades. Here's what he does. To a glass full of water he adds some particular chemical. Then he dilutes the mixture, then dilutes it again, then dilutes it again, then again, continuing until he has a glass full of nothing but absolutely pristine water. (You do much the same every day when you wash a glass with soapy water, then rinse it repeatedly till there's no soap left.) The pristine water in the glass, says Jacques Benveniste, remembers what the old water molecules told it: that once there was another chemical in that glass.

Benveniste's 1988 paper in *Nature* caused a first-class hoo-ha. To most scientists, the notion that "water has a memory" sounded nonsensical. But it was a big new idea, and scientists love nothing better than to try out the latest big new idea. And so thousands of scientists around the world did try. And, except for a few ardent advocates of homeopathic medicine, none of them could make it work. After wasting their time, some were disgusted, others amused. The biology magazine *The Scientist* reported that:

"Some scientists have had the good sense to turn to wit instead of spleen ... Take NIH's Henry Metzger who tried unsuccessfully to duplicate Benveniste's finding that water retains a 'memory' of molecules it once contained. 'It's a shame,' Metzger sighs. 'It still takes a full teaspoon of sugar to sweeten our tea.'"

In 1991, for his insight that water has memory, Jacques Benveniste won the very first Ig Nobel Prize in the field of Chemistry. Not long afterward, Linus Pauling, the only man who won two undivided

Nobel Prizes (one for Chemistry, one for Peace), told the Ig Nobel Board of Governors that he hoped Edward Teller, winner of that year's Ig Nobel Peace Prize (see the section of this book on Edward Teller, "Father of the Bomb") would become the first man to have two Ig Nobel Prizes. But Pauling's hope was not realized.

Benveniste kept doing experiments, publishing papers (generally in obscure places), and ridiculing those who questioned his claims.

Eventually he left INSERM (press reports were vague about whether he left by choice) and moved to his own company, Digital Biology Laboratory, which he says will one day be bigger than Microsoft.

At Digital Biology Laboratory, Benveniste has been working to become the new Thomas Edison and the new Bill Gates combined. As Edison recorded memories from people, Benveniste is recording memories from water. Once he has these memories in digital format, they can be transmitted over telephone lines or over the Internet. Soon, according to Benveniste, pharmacists will stop selling drugs that are pills or liquids. Instead, prescriptions will be filled by, essentially, connecting a telephone line to your glass of water. Digital Biology Laboratory expects to be the leader of an entirely transformed pharmaceutical industry, and so to make Jacques Benveniste very, very wealthy.

In 1997, Benveniste filed a lawsuit against three prominent French scientists, two of them Nobel Laureates, who publicly expressed doubt about his work. The lawsuit was thrown out of court in 1988. Later that year, Jacques Benveniste became the first person to be awarded a second Ig Nobel Prize. This time around, he was honored for his discovery that watery memories can be transmitted by telephone and over the Internet.

The winner could not, or would not, attend the Ig Nobel Prize Ceremony, either in 1991 or in 1998. At the 1998 ceremony, both the magician James Randi and the chemist Dudley Herschbach (see box opposite) gave personal tributes to Benveniste.

At his laboratory in France, Benveniste told a reporter from *Nature* magazine he was "happy to receive a second Ig Nobel Prize, because it shows that those making the awards don't understand anything. People don't give out Nobel Prizes without first trying to find out what the recipients are doing. But the people who give out Ig Nobels don't even bother to inquire about the work."

The *Nature* report concludes with this paragraph:

"Harvard chemist Dudley Herschbach, who won the 1986 Nobel Prize in Chemistry, finds Benveniste's claims 'very hard to reconcile with what we know about molecules.' Herschbach considers the second 'Ig' prize 'very well deserved. And he just might win a third one if he keeps going in this way.' "

The Ig Nobel Prizes

A FLOWING PERSONAL TRIBUTE

Here is Nobel Laureate Dudley Herschbach's moving tribute to two-time Ig winner Jacques Benveniste, delivered at the 1998 Ig Nobel Prize Ceremony.

"Immortal science, like great art, opens new perspectives on nature. Jacques Benveniste did so in 1988, when he published an astonishing article in *Nature* magazine. It reported his conclusion that water, once having encountered a biologically active molecule, remembered the experience very well—so well that long afterward it could transmit the characteristic biological activity. The resonance with another classic of French literature—Proust's *Remembrance of Things Passed* [sic]—was uncanny.

"I must admit I was initially skeptical of his new work. It seemed quite incredible that specific biological activity could be transmitted by telephone or by the Internet. But Benveniste reports he has done thousands of experiments, simply by recording in the ordinary audio range signals from water. He does emphasize that, for his method to work, the water must have been 'informed' by receiving vibrations from the appropriate biomolecule. I've read several reports from

(continued)

A FLOWING PERSONAL TRIBUTE (*continued*)

Benveniste's lav—laboratory, which is named the Digital
Biology Lavatory—er, Laboratory.

"The results led me to try some similar experiments with
vibrating water—water that I was certain had indeed been
informed of biological activity and might have remembrance
of things passed. I have recorded these experiments, and now
transmit them to you. [At this point, Professor Herschbach
played a tape recording of a toilet being flushed.] I trust you
heard that.

"These experiments, which you can easily replicate,
indicate that although Benveniste's remarkable work may not
imitate nature, it certainly offers a new perspective on the call
of nature."

DISCOVERIES—
THINGS THAT RISE OR FALL

 The fall of mankind, perhaps from toilets, raises many questions. So does the fall of certain objects and the rise of others. Here are four investigations of things that lifted or plunged:

- Injuries Due to Falling Coconuts
- The Fall of Buttered Toast
- The Collapse of Toilets in Glasgow
- Levitating Frogs

INJURIES DUE TO FALLING COCONUTS

THE OFFICIAL CITATION

THE IG NOBEL MEDICINE PRIZE WAS AWARDED TO

Peter Barss of McGill University, for his impactful medical report, "Injuries Due to Falling Coconuts."

His study was published in *The Journal of Trauma*, vol. 21, no. 11, 1984, pp. 90–1.

As a young Canadian doctor newly arrived in Papua, New Guinea, Peter Barss wondered what were the most common kinds of injuries that brought people to the Provincial Hospital in Alotau, Milne Bay Province. A surprisingly high percentage of these injuries, he discovered, were due to falling coconuts.

A relatively small number of people are actually killed by falling coconuts. One was the case of:

"A man who had come down to visit the coast from his home in the mountains of the island, where there are few palm trees. He was perhaps unaware of the dangers of falling coconuts. He was standing beneath a tree as another man kicked down a coconut. It struck him squarely on the top of his skull; he dropped, and died within a few minutes."

Coconut palms, Dr. Barss points out, grow to a great height. This is particularly true of the *Cocos nucifera,* variety typica, the most common type in Milne Bay Province.

"The trees grow continuously in height for 80 to 100 years, commonly reach 24 to 30 meters, and can be as high as 35 meters. The coconuts are attached high up in bunches at the top of the trunk . . . They are sometimes harvested green for drinking, which is done by climbing the tree and cutting, kicking, or pulling loose the coconuts. [Dry coconuts] sometimes fall during heavy wind or during prolonged rainfall when the weight of the husks may increase. Houses are often built close to coconut palms. It is not surprising that adults or children are occasionally struck by falling nuts."

Dr. Barss's report includes the first thoroughgoing technical analysis of the unfettered descent of a coconut (see overleaf). Important and interesting though the physics may be, the report's greatest import, like that of a falling coconut, is on the health of ordinary people. Dr. Barss's hard-hitting conclusion says:

"The physical forces involved in a direct blow to the skull by a falling coconut are potentially very large. Glancing blows will, of course, be less serious. It seems unwise to locate dwellings near coconut palms, and children should not be allowed to play under coconut trees with mature nuts."

Dr. Barss has, in his career, treated many kinds of injuries, some peculiar to the parts of the world in which he was living at the time. Visitors to what are, for them, far-off climes would do well to consult the medical literature for a quick heads up on what to watch out for when they arrive. Dr. Barss has published more than 40 medical reports, including several about illnesses and injuries characteristic of the South Pacific. These include: "Injuries Caused by Pigs in Papua New Guinea" (*Medical Journal of Australia*, vol. 149, December 5–19, 1988, pp. 649–56); "Grass-Skirt Burns in Papua New Guinea" (*The Lancet*, 1983); "Penetrating Wounds Caused by Needle-Fish in Oceania" (*Medical Journal of Australia*, 1985); and "Inhalation Hazards of Tropical 'Pea Shooters'" (*Papua and New Guinea Medical Journal*, 1985).

All of these are real and present dangers. But it is for looking into the matter of injuries due to falling coconuts—and for doing something about them—that Peter Barss won the 2001 Ig Nobel Prize in the field of Medicine.

Dr. Barss traveled, at his own expense, from Montreal to the Ig Nobel Prize Ceremony. In accepting the Prize, he showed slides and said:

"I did this work in Papua New Guinea. I brought a few pictures of the wonderful people I worked with that helped me do my research. These are the type of trees people fall from . . . and this is a man with a spinal cord injury falling from a tree being taken away . . . Most of these people die, unfortunately. This is a simple device for removing breadfruit from a tree, to prevent injuries . . . This one is just a simple prevention measure of pruning mango trees so you don't have to climb so high and fall so hard. Some of the heights of tropical trees are about the same as 10-story buildings, so the mass of a falling coconut is about a metric ton with a direct hit. So, the worst place to be when a coconut falls, is asleep under the tree. Because your head is on the ground and you have a zero, uh, stopping distance so the physicists know the kinetic energy is infinite. It's better to be standing up and get knocked down . . ." (At this point, Miss Sweetie Poo terminated Dr. Barss's speech.)

The Ig Nobel Prizes

TECHNICAL ANALYSIS OF A FALLING COCONUT

Here is Peter Barss's description of the Newtonian mechanics of a free-falling coconut:

"An average unhusked, mature dry coconut may weigh from 1 to more than 2 kilograms (2.2–4.4 pounds). A nut whose husk is soaked with water, or a green coconut, can weigh as much as 4 kilograms (8.8 pounds). When such a mass is accelerated by gravity, after falling from a height approximately equal to a 10-story building, and then comes to rest by being suddenly decelerated onto someone's head, it is not surprising that severe head injuries sometimes occur. If a

(continued)

TECHNICAL ANALYSIS OF A FALLING COCONUT
(continued)

coconut weighing 2 kilograms (4.4 pounds) falls 25 meters onto a person's head, the impact velocity is 80 kilometers (50 miles)/hour. The decelerating force on the head will vary depending on whether a direct or glancing blow is received. The distance in which the coconut is decelerated is also an important factor. Thus an infant's head lying on the ground would receive a much greater force than that received by the head of a standing adult, that dropped as it was struck. For a stopping distance of 5 centimeters (2 inches) and a direct blow, the force would be 1,000 kilograms (2,205 pounds)."

THE FALL OF BUTTERED TOAST

THE OFFICIAL CITATION
THE IG NOBEL PHYSICS PRIZE WAS AWARDED TO

Robert Matthews of Aston University, England, for his studies of Murphy's Law, and especially for demonstrating that toast often falls on the buttered side.

His study was published as "Tumbling Toast, Murphy's Law and the Fundamental Constants," *European Journal of Physics*, vol. 16, no. 4, July 18, 1995, pp. 172–6. Details of the later empirical test were published in *School Science Review*, vol. 83, 2001, pp. 23–8.

The fall of buttered toast is, among other things, an old joke. In 1844, the poet and satirist James Payn wrote:

> I've never had a piece of toast
> particularly long and wide,
> but fell upon a sanded floor,
> and always on the buttered-side.

More than a century later someone (there is much dispute as to who) pointed out that if cats always land on their feet, you could strap buttered toast onto the back of a cat, and the combination might spin forever, suspended inches above the ground.

In 1995, Robert Matthews strapped mathematics onto the buttered toast question, and out dropped a revelation.

* * *

Matthews is a chartered physicist, a fellow of the Royal Astronomical Society, and a fellow of the Royal Statistical Society. He is a student of Murphy's Law. He took the toast question seriously.

There are many factors that must be considered. Matthews began by demolishing a cherished assumption:

"There is a widespread belief," he wrote, "that it is the result of a genuine physical asymmetry induced by one side of the toast being buttered . . . This explanation cannot be correct. The mass of butter added to toast (on the order of 4 grams, $\frac{1}{6}$ oz) is small compared to the mass of the typical slice of toast (on the order of 35 grams, $1\frac{1}{4}$ oz), is thinly spread, and passes into the body of the toast. Its contribution to the total moment of inertia of the toast—and thus its effect on the toast's rotational dynamics—is thus negligible."

Then, in a mere five pages of computation, Matthews explored the behavior of a rigid, rough, homogeneous rectangular lamina, mass m, side $2a$, falling from a rigid platform set a height h above the ground. He considered the dynamics of this body from an initial state where this center of gravity overhangs the table by a distance *delta subnought*, and analyzed it mercilessly through all stages of its perilous journey to the final resting position at height h equals zero.

When he had finished, there was a startling insight:

"The formula giving the maximum height of humans turns out to contain three so-called fundamental constants of the universe. The first—the electromagnetic fine-structure constant—determines the strength of the chemical bonds in the skull, while the second—the gravitational fine-structure constant—determines the strength of gravity. Finally, the so-called Bohr radius dictates the size of atoms making up the body. The precise values of these three fundamental constants were built into the very design of the universe just moments after the Big Bang. In other words, toast falling off the breakfast table lands butter-side down because the universe is made that way."

This, of course, did not end the controversy—Murphy's Law forbids that ever happening. After Robert Matthews published his paper, other scientists leaped yackettingly into the arena. They quibbled furiously about parametric values, the calculus of variations, and certain fine points of stochastic estimation methodology. No matter. Matthews had produced a standard against which all crumby researchers, now and forever, must measure their work.

For adding a thick dollop of mathematics to a smear of butter and a slice of toast, Robert Matthews won the 1996 Ig Nobel Prize in the field of Physics.

The winner could not travel to the Ig Nobel Prize Ceremony, but instead sent an audiotaped acceptance speech. True to Murphy's Law, the tape arrived at Harvard four days after the ceremony. In the speech, Dr. Matthews said:

"Thank you very much for this award. Proving that Murphy's Law—if something can go wrong, it will—is built into the design of the universe has brought me, as one of the most pessimistic people on earth, a lot of pleasure, and so has this Ig Nobel Prize. There is, of course, a more serious side to my work, I just can't remember what it is. Oh, yes, I know. I should get out more."

Matthews thereafter continued his research both on matters covered by Murphy's Law and on other practical questions outside the law. Why there are so many odd socks in our drawers; why rope or string so often seems to acquire knots; why places you're looking for so often lie in awkward places on maps; whether to take an umbrella following a forecast of rain; whether to switch queues while waiting in a supermarket—Robert Matthews has attacked all these and more with dash, vim, and stylish mathematics.

In 2001, he returned to the question of buttered toast. Having already solved it theoretically, he now attacked the problem empirically. That is to say, he conducted an experiment:

"A total of just over 1,000 schoolchildren (70% primary, 30% secondary) from schools across the UK took part in the three experiments, performing a total of over 21,000 drops of toast. The dedication of some of the school teams was impressive, with 22 reporting at least 100 drops, 10 at least 400 drops, and two conducting over 1,000. The overall results of the three basic experiments were as follows:

"Out of a total of 9,821 drops, there were 6,101 butter-down landings, a rate of 62%, which is 12% higher than the 50% rate expected if—as many scientists have claimed—toast is as likely to land butter-up as down, and its final state is random."

And thus Robert Matthews demonstrated, both theoretically and experimentally, that nature abhors a newly vacuumed floor.

THE COLLAPSE OF
TOILETS IN GLASGOW

THE OFFICIAL CITATION
THE IG NOBEL PUBLIC HEALTH PRIZE WAS AWARDED TO
Jonathan Wyatt, Gordon McNaughton, and William Tullet of
Glasgow, for their alarming report, "The Collapse of Toilets in
Glasgow."

**Their study was published in the _Scottish Medical Journal,_ vol. 38, 1993,
p. 185.**

Three doctors working in the Department of Accident and Emergency of the Western Infirmary in Glasgow noticed an unusual con-
junction of events: "three patients who presented during a period of
six months with injuries sustained whilst sitting on toilets which unexpectedly collapsed."

This, they decided, was worth investigating.

The three reports were, upon reexamination, remarkably dissimilar.

The first involved a 14-year-old girl who weighed 83 kilograms
(183 lbs), who "sustained a 7-centimeter (3-inch) wound to the posterior aspect of her right thigh when she sat on a school toilet which
promptly collapsed."

The second was a 34-year-old man who weighed 70 kilograms
(154 lbs), who "sustained a 6-centimeter (2.5-inch) wound to his
right buttock when a toilet collapsed under him during defecation."

The third patient was a 48-year-old man who weighed 76 kilograms (168 lbs), who was "sitting on a toilet which disintegrated,
causing multiple wounds to both buttocks."

In all three cases, the collapse was of the porcelain lavatory pan, not of the toilet seats. The official report says that "the exact ages and origins of the pans were not known, but all were described as white porcelain."

In each case, the attending physician cleansed and sutured the wound under local anesthetic, and the patient went on to make a full recovery.

Drs. Wyatt, McNaughton, and Tullet conclude their report with a grim, but not entirely discouraging, summary, and a practical suggestion:

"The toilet collapses described in this study, whilst not producing life-threatening injuries, resulted in considerable embarrassment and discomfort for those involved. Toilet collapse appears to be unusual; a literature search failed to reveal any previous similar reports. The cause remains unclear, except that all of the toilets were believed to be very old. We would therefore advise that the older porcelain familiar to so many of us should be treated with a certain degree of

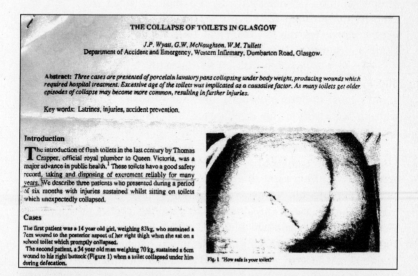

THE COLLAPSE OF TOILETS IN GLASGOW

J.P. Wyatt, G.W. McNaughton, W.M. Tullett
Department of Accident and Emergency, Western Infirmary, Dumbarton Road, Glasgow.

Abstract: *Three cases are presented of porcelain lavatory pans collapsing under body weight, producing wounds which required hospital treatment. Excessive age of the toilets was implicated as a causative factor. As many toilets get older episodes of collapse may become more common, resulting in further injuries.*

Key words: Latrines, injuries, accident prevention.

Introduction

The introduction of flush toilets in the last century by Thomas Crapper, official royal plumber to Queen Victoria, was a major advance in public health.[1] These toilets havo a good safety record, taking and disposing of excrement reliably for many years. We describe three patients who presented during a period of six months with injuries sustained whilst sitting on toilets which unexpectedly collapsed.

Cases

The first patient was a 14 year old girl, weighing 83kg, who sustained a 7cm wound to the posterior aspect of her right thigh when she sat on a school toilet which promptly collapsed.

The second patient, a 34 year old man weighing 70 kg, sustained a 6cm wound to his right buttock (Figure 1) when a toilet collapsed under him during defecation.

Fig. 1 "How safe is your toilet?"

Wyatt, McNaughton, and Tullet's Prize-winning paper.

caution. An obvious way of using a toilet without fear of it collapsing is to take a continental approach and not to sit down, but to adopt a hovering stance above it."

For their contributions to the safety and peace of mind of the populace of greater Glasgow, Jonathan Wyatt, Gordon McNaughton, and William Tullet won the 2000 Ig Nobel Prize in the field of Public Health.

Jonathan Wyatt and Gordon McNaughton traveled, at their own expense, from Glasgow to the Ig Nobel Prize Ceremony. Mc-Naughton wore a kilt for the occasion. Wyatt did not. In accepting the Prize, they kept their remarks short and to the point:

Jonathan Wyatt: "Thank you very much, ladies and gentlemen, it's a wonderful honor to be here tonight. You won't believe it, but our research has previously been dismissed as a mere flush in the pan. But this ceremony has been able to show it in its true light. Gordon—this is Gordon here, from Scotland—would particularly like to thank you for your American hospitality. Just to explain, for those of you who don't understand why it is that Scotsmen wear kilts, he's been trying out your toilets and he finds it very easy with this particular kilt to try out a number of toilets and, so far, so good. I'll hand you on to Gordon. Thank you very much."

Gordon McNaughton: "To link in with tonight's intelligence theme, we thought it would be an opportunity to mention one of England's most famous plumbers, and that is Mister Thomas Crapper, who, in fact, without his intelligence and his invention of the flush toilet, we would not be standing here today. Thank you very much."

Two months after the ceremony, the Ig Nobel Board of Governors received a note from a Mr. Alasdair Baxter of Nottingham, England, which read as follows:

"Do pardon this intrusive E-mail but I have a sneaking feeling that I could be one of the victims of a collapsing toilet mentioned in the research paper published in the *Scottish Medical Journal*, vol. 38, 1993, p. 185. While working as a temporary schoolteacher in Coatbridge near Glasgow in August 1971, I sat on a toilet in the school which collapsed and caused severe lacerations of my buttocks and back. Sadly, I cannot get ready access to the *Scottish Medical Jour-*

nal to check it out and if you can send me a copy of the article, I shall be very grateful indeed. Alternatively, if you have an E-mail address for either Dr. Wyatt or Dr. McNaughton, I shall E-mail them directly. Thank you in anticipation."

The Board sent a copy of Mr. Baxter's note to Dr. McNaughton. Dr. McNaughton replied with the bittersweet news that Mr. Baxter's buttocks were not amongst those which he, Dr. Wyatt, and Dr. Tullet had had the honor of examining.

LEVITATING FROGS

THE OFFICIAL CITATION
THE IG NOBEL PHYSICS PRIZE WAS AWARDED TO

Andre Geim of the University of Nijmegen, the Netherlands, and Sir Michael Berry of Bristol University, England, for using magnets to levitate a frog.

Their study was published as "Of Flying Frogs and Levitrons," *European Journal of Physics,* **vol. 18, 1997, pp. 307–13. Andre Geim's Web site (www.hfml.sci.kun.nl/froglev.html) has short videos of the frog, a cricket, a strawberry, and a drop of water being levitated.**

"No, you cannot magnetize a frog," is the conclusion most scientists would have reached had they ever given a thought to the question, "Can you magnetize a frog?" Most scientists should consider themselves fortunate, because had they considered the question, and reached that conclusion, and publicly staked their reputation on saying so, they would have been dead wrong.

The frog levitation was a one-man tour de force. The theoretical underpinnings were a joint effort. Michael Berry explains:

"The flying frog was Andre Geim's experiment. I was told about it after giving a lecture on the physics of the levitron—a toy in which a magnetized spinning top floats above a magnetized base. It seemed that the flying frog and the floating top ought to depend on similar physical principles, so I got in touch with Andre. Then we worked together, to extend to the frog the explanation I had previously found for the levitron.

"It is surprising at first to see the frog suspended in midair, in apparent defiance of gravity. It is supported by the force of magnetism. The force comes from a powerful electromagnet. It is able to push upward on the frog because the frog is a magnet, too, albeit a weak one. The frog is intrinsically nonmagnetic but becomes magnetized by the field of the electromagnet—this is called 'induced diamagnetism.' Most substances are diamagnetic, and Andre was able to levitate a variety of objects, including drops of water and hazelnuts.

"In principle, a person could be magnetically levitated too—like frogs, we are mostly water. The field would not have to be stronger, but would have to fill the much larger volume of a person, and that

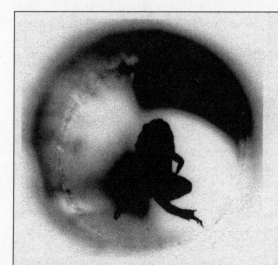

Figure 4(b). Frog levitated in the stable region.

A variety of diamagnetic objects was inserted into the magnet, and the current through the coils adjusted until stable levitation occurred (figure 4(b)). The corresponding fields B_0 were all close to the calculated 16 T, and the objects always floated near the top of the

Of course this represen
currents localized in a
charge, so the living
Indeed, they emerged
without suffering any n
also Schenck (1992) ar

As we showed earl
paramagnets stably.
be achieved, and from
clear that this occurs fo
of the solenoid—rather
$\chi_{paramagnetic} \approx 10^{-3} \approx$
vertically stable but la
some paramagnetic obj
stainless steel, parama
were suspended in thi
were held against the
a few occasions, paran
contact, but were foun
current of paramagneti
for example by coverir
gauze, the objects slipp
against the wall.

6. Discussion

Our treatment of diam

has not been achieved yet. I have no reason to believe such levitation would be a harmful or painful experience, but of course nobody can be sure of this. Nevertheless, I would enthusiastically volunteer to be the first levitatee.

"The tricky part of the physics is to understand why the equilibrium of the frog is stable—that is, why it remains suspended. Most physicists would—mistakenly—expect the frog to slip sideways out of the field, and fall (an analogy is the instability of a pencil balancing on its point). This wrong expectation is based on a theorem proved by Samuel Earnshaw in 1842: no stationary object can be held stably by magnetism and gravity alone. But the frog is not stationary. There is the circulation of electrons in the creature's atoms. These are small effects, but they mean that Earnshaw's theorem does not strictly apply, and this opens the possibility that the equilibrium can be stable.

"The trick is to get the forces to balance in these regions. If you get it wrong, the frog will fall."

For their magnetic levity, Andre Geim and Michael Berry won the 2000 Ig Nobel Prize in the field of Physics.

Andre Geim flew at his own expense from Nijmegen, the Netherlands, to the Ig Nobel Prize Ceremony. In accepting the Prize, he said:

"Our story contains some unappreciated knowledge about magnetism. We want to accept this prize also on behalf of the hundreds who wrote to us with their ideas. The enquiries came from engineers who wanted to use levitation for everything from waste recycling and materials processing, to levitating sports shoes and jewelry in shop windows; from our physicist colleagues, some of whom admitted that after learning about the frog they finally understood some of their old results; from chemists and biologists who did not want to wait for a space shuttle and realized they could do microgravity experiments in a magnet; from servicemen to pensioners and from prisoners to priests. Sometimes, their ideas were bright and unexpected, sometimes goofy, sometimes ridiculous or, even mad, but always creative. Even more rewarding were letters from children all over the world who wrote 'I am nine years old and want to become a scientist.'" (Dr. Geim continued for a short while longer, but Miss Sweetie Poo, who herself was eight years old, terminated his speech.)

TROY AND THE GRIZZLY BEAR

 Of all the Ig Nobel Prize winners, one defies all efforts to categorize him. Troy Hurtubise rates a chapter entirely of his own. Here, in brief, is the story of:

- Troy and the Grizzly Bear

TROY AND THE GRIZZLY BEAR

THE OFFICIAL CITATION
THE IG NOBEL SAFETY ENGINEERING PRIZE WAS AWARDED TO

Troy Hurtubise, of North Bay, Ontario, for developing and personally testing a suit of armor that is impervious to grizzly bears.

Troy Hurtubise and his work are shown in the documentary film *Project Grizzly*, produced by the National Film Board of Canada. Further information and video clips are on Troy's Web site, www. projecttroy.com.

At age 20, out alone panning for gold in the Canadian wilderness, Troy Hurtubise had an encounter of some sort with a grizzly bear. Troy has devoted the rest of his life to creating a grizzly bear–proof suit of armor in which he could safely go and commune with that bear. The suit's basic design was influenced by the powerful humanoid-policeman-robot-from-the-future title character in *RoboCop*, a movie Troy happened to see shortly before he began his intensive research and development work.

Troy is a pure example of the lone inventor, in the tradition of James Watt, Thomas Edison, and Nikola Tesla. Regarded by some as a half-genius, by others as a half-crackpot, he has unsurpassed persistence and imagination. Troy also is very careful. The proof that he is very careful is that he is still alive.

A grizzly bear is tremendously, ferociously powerful. Troy realized that he would be wise to test his suit under controlled conditions prior to giving it the ultimate test. He spent seven years and, by his estimate, $150,000 Canadian, subjecting the suit to every large, sudden force he could devise. For almost all of the testing, Troy was locked inside the bulky suit, despite his being severely claustrophobic.

The suit is a technical wonder, especially when one realizes that Troy had to assemble it mostly from scrounged materials. Troy is a natural leader blessed with boundless charisma, charm, and good humor. He works with a team of volunteers, who are ever at the ready to drop whatever they are supposed to be doing and help Troy build and test each new version of his invention. They also help Troy videotape most of the tests. Some of the best early footage was included in the National Film Board of Canada's 1997 documentary *Project Grizzly*. *Project Grizzly* also shows Troy's first sally back into the wilderness, on horseback and with the proper clothing, in search of the bear. The producers promoted the film with a cheery invitation:

"Join Troy as he tests his armour and courage, in stunts that are both hair-raising and hilarious. Journey with this modern-day Don Quixote and his band of men, as they travel from the donut shops and biker bars of North Bay to the mythic Rocky Mountains, for a date with destiny."

Troy enjoyed the attention, but was disappointed that the tone of the movie does not

Troy Hurtubise in his grizzly bear–proof suit of armor. Photo: Greg Pacek, courtesy of the National Film Board of Canada.

properly highlight his commitment to doing research on the science of grizzly bears.

The film does make abundantly clear that Troy does not let setbacks discourage him. One setback came in the late 1990s, when Troy was forced to declare bankruptcy, and the Ontario bankruptcy court took possession of his suit. Since that time, the court has been trying to find a buyer. The court occasionally gives Troy permission to borrow the suit, most commonly for television interviews and other public appearances when a buyer might be likely to see and decide to covet it.

For conceiving of, and building, and testing the suit, and for keeping it and himself intact the whole while, Troy Hurtubise won the 1998 Ig Nobel Prize in the field of Safety Engineering. The Ontario bankruptcy court gave permission for the suit to accompany Troy to the ceremony at Harvard.

Troy traveled from his home in North Bay, Ontario, to the Ig Nobel Prize Ceremony accompanied by his wife, Laurie, and a mysterious man named Brock, who wore a dark business suit, and whom Troy introduced as a court-appointed guardian for the suit, but who described himself as "the president of one of Troy's companies." The three of them had a minor, but not lengthy, adventure getting the suit through American customs inspection at Boston's Logan Airport. From there it was a short trip through Boston traffic, over the Charles River into Cambridge, and finally to Sanders Theatre at Harvard.

In accepting the Prize, Troy said:

"I'm still alive, anyway. What can I say? I'm just a simple man from northern Ontario, standing in the hallowed halls of Harvard. I say, feel the tension, man, what a ride! We must look past the obvious absurdity of some inventions and discoveries, and set aside the narrow-mindedness of science, if for but a moment, to allow the view to become unobstructed, with a vehicle called imagination.

"The Mark VI suit is bulletproof and fireproof, and all those kinds of nice things. The exoskeleton is pure titanium. The outside rubber base protects the electronics. For two years I had a problem of getting them to bond. So to bond the rubber to the titanium, I coated the inside of the suit—which you can't see—with 7,630 feet of duct tape.

"Tomorrow, at the Science Center at Harvard, I will unveil, as a world exclusive, the next prototype—the G-Man Genesis—and the science behind it." ·

The next day, Troy revealed—for the first time anywhere, and before an eager press of reporters and technologists—his plans for the next-generation suit. Estimated to cost $1.5 million in its first incarnation, the G-Man Genesis, he said, will be lighter, stronger, and far more maneuverable than its predecessor. A person wearing the suit will be able to run at full tilt, and to explore inside volcanoes.

That evening, Troy appeared at two special public screenings of *Project Grizzly* at the Harvard's Carpenter Center before sold-out, adoring crowds.

Troy returned to Harvard the following year, to help honor the new crop of Ig Nobel Prize winners, and also to lecture at MIT, where he brought a roomful of engineers to a near frenzy of inspiration.

Since then, Troy has continued to do advanced research and development work, and to have unexpected adventures involving, among other things, NASA, the National Hockey League, an invention to separate oil from sand, a tapped phone, a mysterious nocturnal break-in, getting kicked in the crotch on television by comedian Roseanne Barr, a visit from al-Qaeda hijackers, and an encounter in a locked room with two Kodiak bears.

INVENTIONS

Most inventors, like most of their inventions, draw little public attention. Here are three exceptions:

- The Most Inventive Salesman
- The Kitty and the Keyboard
- Patenting the Wheel

THE MOST INVENTIVE SALESMAN

THE OFFICIAL CITATION
THE IG NOBEL CONSUMER ENGINEERING PRIZE WAS AWARDED TO

Ron Popeil, incessant inventor and perpetual pitchman of late-night television, for redefining the industrial revolution with such devices as the Veg-O-Matic, the Pocket Fisherman, Mr. Microphone, and the Inside-the-Shell Egg Scrambler.

Ron Popeil tells his story in the book *The Salesman of the Century: Inventing, Marketing, and Selling on TV: How I Did It and How You Can Too!*

For more than four decades, American television has been filled with commercials for strange, cheap inventions with curious names—the Buttoneer, the Pocket Fisherman, the Mince-O-Matic, the Inside-the-Shell Egg Scrambler, and nearly countless others.

Behind all of them lay a relentlessly glib, and simply relentless, salesman/inventor named Ron Popeil.

Civilization had produced many inventors of half-needed devices. Civilization had produced many overenergized salesmen. Ron Popeil (he pronounces it "poe-*peel*") is both. The combination is not terribly special, but Ron Popeil, the man, is. More than anyone else, he used television as a super-effective, super-irritating, yet unquestionably compelling way to goose up the process of selling junky little gadgets.

Ron Popeil was born to a clan of inventive, cantankerous salesmen.

Young Ron's father, the inventor/salesman S.J. Popeil, designed and built a thingy called the Chop-O-Matic, "a simple chopping device that cuts up vegetables, potatoes, and meats." S.J. Popeil endured travails for his Chop-O-Matic. He filed a lawsuit against his uncle, the inventor/salesman Nathan Morris, for devising and marketing a similar device called the Roto-Chop. Nathan Morris was a veteran of such battles, chiefly fought against his own brother, the inventor/salesman Al Morris. S.J. Popeil managed to reach a legal settlement with his uncle Nathan, thus freeing the Chop-O-Matic from legal limbo. (Ironically, many years later, S.J. Popeil lost a legal battle with the Swiss inventors of an earlier Chop-O-Matic–like machine called the Blitzhacker.)

Eventually, Ron figured out how to well and truly promote and sell his papa's Chop-O-Matic.

Armed with this heritage, these skills, and this experience, Ron went on to invent or acquire a truly bewildering array of little machines, and advertise, advertise, advertise them down people's throats.

No one exactly needed any of these products, but with their snazzy names the cheap little gizmos were somehow weirdly enticing. Each filled a different need that people *almost* believed they had.

Television ads, cheaply made and cheaply broadcast, were the key to success. Ron Popeil devised ways to inexpensively produce and broadcast his ads again and again, ad nauseam, day and night (especially late night, when it cost him almost nothing to get air time). The sales pitch drilled deep into the nervous system of anyone whose television set happened to be turned on.

Popeil's ads were engineering marvels, as were his product names. Snappy and attention-grabbing, each commercial had a high-pressure announcer who dispensed a stream of rat-a-tat patter, harping on the product name. Full of cloyingly artificial friendliness, the announcer repeated the pitch several times, always sweetening the deal with idiotic little extras. "But wait," he would say, "there's more!"

What were the inventions?

- The INSTANT-SHINE—shoeshine spray.
- The PLASTIC PLANT KIT—which consisted of "tubes of liquid plastic in a variety of leafy colors along with an assortment of metal plates with inverted leaf designs, stems, and green tape."
- DIAL-O-MATIC—food slicer—"You slice through a tomato so thin, you can read a newspaper through it."
- The VEG-O-MATIC—"Slices and dices and juliennes to perfection. Slice a whole potato into uniform slices with one motion. Simply turn the ring and change from thin to thick slices. Like magic you can change from slicing to dicing. No one likes dicing onions. The Veg-O-Matic makes mounds of them fast. The only tears you'll shed will be tears of joy."
- The MINCE-O-MATIC—"With powerful vacuum grip!" Customers who bought one also got a "free" bonus: the Food Glamorizer, "which can make fresh lemon-peel twists fast like a bartender."
- The BUTTONEER—"The problem with buttons is that they always fall off. And when they do, don't sew them on the old-fashioned way with needle and thread. Use the Buttoneer!"
- The RONCO SMOKELESS ASHTRAY—When you put a cigarette in the ashtray, the smoke is sucked into a filtering system.
- MR. MICROPHONE—A simple wireless microphone that could broadcast to any nearby FM radio. "It's practical and great fun for the whole family, and it's only $14.88. Buy two or three, they make really great gifts!"
- The INSIDE THE OUTSIDE WINDOW WASHER—This product didn't sell too well.
- The TRIM-COMB—A small plastic comb with a razor blade inside of it. "Now anyone can trim hair and eliminate costly haircuts. It trims, thins, shapes, blends, and tapers. All you do is comb."
- The RONCO BOTTLE AND JAR CUTTER—"An exciting new way to recycle throwaway bottles and jars into decorative glassware, centerpieces, thousands of things . . . A hobby for Dad, craft for the kids, a great gift for Mom. The Ronco Bottle and Jar Cutter. Only $7.77."
- The POPEIL POCKET FISHERMAN—"Want to make a boy happy? Give him the Pocket Fisherman."

- The RONCO 5-TRAY ELECTRIC FOOD DEHYDRATOR—"A device for producing beef jerky, banana chips, soup mix, and even pot-pourri at home."
- The HULA HOE—"The weeder with a wiggle."
- CELLUTROL—"The beauty aid for buttocks, hips, and thighs."
- The GLH (Great Looking Hair!) FORMULA NUMBER 9 HAIR SYSTEM—Spray-on paint that covers bald spots.

In 1991 and 1993, Popeil obtained patents (US #5,017,143 and US #5,221,962) for new ways to produce subliminal advertising messages on television screens.

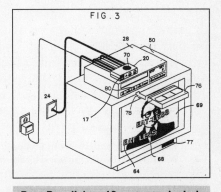

Ron Popeil has 13 patents, including two for producing subliminal images on television screens. This is a technical drawing from US Patent #5,221,962, "Subliminal Device Having Manual Adjustment of Perception Level of Subliminal Messages."

In his autobiography, Ron Popeil described the mystique of the inventor:

"We're celebrities, folk heroes, the common man (or woman) who has made good. Being an inventor (even if you're really [just] an innovator) seems to give you credibility. What's even better is if you can invent, innovate, and market. The combination of the three is sure to make you a media celebrity."

The autobiography begins with a simple thought that characterizes Popeil's spirit and his many fine inventions:

"I pushed. I yelled. I hawked."

And it worked. "I was stuffing money into my pockets, more money than I had ever seen in my life."

For his years of ceaseless invention, Ron Popeil won the 1993 Ig Nobel Prize in the field of Consumer Engineering.

The winner could not, or would not, attend the Ig Nobel Prize Ceremony. He carried on with his life's work of inventing and selling.

THE KITTY AND THE KEYBOARD

THE OFFICIAL CITATION
THE IG NOBEL COMPUTER SCIENCE PRIZE WAS AWARDED TO

Chris Niswander of Tucson, Arizona, for inventing PawSense, software that detects when a cat is walking across your computer keyboard.

PawSense is available from BitBoost Systems, 421 E. Drachman, Tucson, AZ 85705, USA (http://www.bitboost.com).

Chris Niswander (pronounced "nice-wander") is a computer scientist who is also editor of the Tucson Mensa Society newsletter. He took an intellectual approach to the fundamental cat/computer problem. First he stated the problem:

"When cats walk or climb on your keyboard, they can enter random commands and data, damage your files, and even crash your computer. This can happen whether you are near the computer or have suddenly been called away from it."

Having stated the problem, he then solved it. In Mr. Niswander's words:

"PawSense is a software utility that helps protect your computer from cats. It quickly detects and blocks cat typing, and also helps train your cat to stay off the computer keyboard."

What people always want to know, after they ask "Why?" is "How does it work?"

* * *

Mr. Niswander always answers the first question politely. Then he explains that "PawSense detects cat typing by weighing a combination of factors to achieve maximal speed and reliability. It analyzes keypress timings and combinations to distinguish cat typing from human typing. PawSense normally recognizes a cat on the keyboard within one or two pawsteps."

When PawSense detects a cat on the keyboard, it takes action, unleashing a blast of loud harmonica music. Alternatively, it unleashes a loud recording of Mr. Niswander hissing, or one of several other sounds which some humans may find delightful, but most cats will not.

Mr. Niswander says that the sounds are not effective against deaf cats, but that once a cat has been recognized, PawSense blocks the cat's keyboard input. In that event, it puts up a giant message on the computer screen: "CAT-LIKE TYPING DETECTED" and requests that you, or the cat, type the word "human." An illiterate cat might beat the system through a lucky combination of paw blows, but its odds of doing so are low.

Mr. Niswander has submitted a patent application for PawSense. He says he plans a second product called "BabySense," but that it requires an indeterminate amount of research and development, and so he is reluctant to name a date on which it will be available. For the meantime, he offers this advice to PawSense customers who want at least partial protection against their little progeny:

PawSense indicates that a cat is at work on the computer keyboard.

"If your baby bangs away with outstretched or open hands, or with fists, that makes keypress patterns close enough to those of cat paws, so PawSense should work relatively well. If your baby carefully pecks at only one key at a time, PawSense will recognize that your baby is indeed a human."

For protecting computers

from feline catastrophe, and, as a bonus, giving minimal protection against babies, Chris Niswander won the 2000 Ig Nobel Prize in the field of Computer Science.

Mr. Niswander traveled, at his own expense, from Tucson, Arizona, to the Ig Nobel Prize Ceremony. In accepting the Prize, he said:

"I'd like to thank my sister's cat, Phobos, for persuading me that this was a really, really good idea. I guess that's all I have to say. Thanks, Phobos, for persuading me that this was a really good idea."

When Mr. Niswander had finished speaking, Mr. Leonid Hambro took elegant possession of the stage to deliver a personal tribute. Mr. Hambro is the former principal pianist for the New York Philharmonic Orchestra, and for 10 years after that he was the touring partner of pianist/comedian Victor Borge. The number he chose to play for this special occasion: Zez Confrey's 1921 composition *Kitten on the Keys*.

PATENTING
THE WHEEL

THE OFFICIAL CITATION
THE IG NOBEL TECHNOLOGY PRIZE WAS AWARDED JOINTLY TO

John Keogh of Hawthorn, Victoria, Australia, for patenting the wheel in the year 2001, and to the Australian Patent Office, for granting him Innovation Patent #2001100012.

"Melbourne Man Patents the Wheel," screamed the headline in the July 2, 2001, issue of the Australian newspaper *The Age.* The article told how this came about:

"A Melbourne man has patented the wheel. Freelance patent attorney John Keogh was issued with an Innovation Patent for a 'circular transportation facilitation device' within days of the new patent system being invoked in May.

"But he has no immediate plans to patent fire, crop rotation or other fundamental advances in civilization. Mr. Keogh said he patented the wheel to prove the innovation patent system was flawed because it did not need to be examined by the patent office, IP Australia.

"'The patent office would be required to issue a patent for anything,' he said. 'All they're doing is putting a rubber stamp on it. The impetus came from the Federal Government. Their constituents claimed the cost of obtaining a patent was too high so the government decided to find a way to issue a patent more easily.'"

The patent office describes the two types of patents granted in Australia:

- A *standard patent* gives long-term protection and control over an invention for up to 20 years.
- An *innovation patent* is a relatively fast, inexpensive protection option available from IP Australia, and is the most recent in a range of other intellectual property rights. Protection lasts for a maximum of eight years.

The patent office states that "The estimated cost of an Australian standard patent including attorney fees is about $5,000 to $8,000." An innovation patent costs $180.

Mr. Keogh obtained an innovation patent. Specifically, he obtained Innovation Patent #2001100012. Officially, his invention is called "a circular transportation facilitation device."

Commissioner of Patents Vivienne Thom has been quoted as saying, "to obtain the patent the applicant must make a declaration that they are the inventor. Obtaining a patent for a wheel would require a false claim, which is a very serious matter and would certainly invalidate the patent as well as amount to a misrepresentation on the part of the applicant and unprofessional conduct by any professional adviser."

The patent office's Web site (*www.IPAustralia.gov.au*) advises patent applicants to examine the records of patents already on file. "Don't reinvent the wheel," says the Web page. "Searching worldwide patent information can help you avoid wasting time and money duplicating work done elsewhere."

For being the first to patent the wheel in the 21st century, John Keogh won the 2001 Ig Nobel Prize in the field of Technology; and for permitting him to do it, the Australian Patent Office shared the honor.

The winners could not, or would not, attend the Ig Nobel Prize Ceremony, but John Keogh did prepare and send a videotaped acceptance speech. In it, he said:

"When I sat down to write the patent specification for the wheel, I had one objective in mind: to expose a key weakness in Australia's

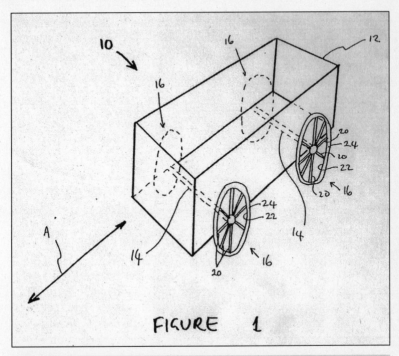

Figure 1 A technical drawing from the patent: "A perspective drawing of a cart incorporating a series of circular transportation facilitation devices in accordance with a preferred aspect of the present invention."

new innovation patent system, which requires the Australian Patent Office to grant a patent for virtually any thing that is applied for. The winning of an Ig Nobel Prize was not an outcome I foresaw. Obtaining a patent for the wheel has had some positive outcomes. The grant of the patent attracted publicity, both within Australia and around the world, highlighting a significant issue in our intellectual property laws. I can only hope that the awarding of the Prize contributes to the push to amend Australian patent laws to ensure the wheel will not again be patented."

HELLISH TECHNICALITIES

In the race for Ig Nobel Prizes, there is one field in which the US dominates, with all other countries struggling— and in many cases failing even to struggle—to compete.

This chapter describes two Prize-winning achievements in the technical study of hell.

- Who Is Going to Hell
- Mikhail Gorbachev Is the Antichrist

WHO IS GOING TO HELL

THE OFFICIAL CITATION
THE IG NOBEL MATHEMATICS PRIZE WAS AWARDED TO

The Southern Baptist Church of Alabama, mathematical measurers of morality, for their county-by-county estimate of how many Alabama citizens will go to hell if they don't repent.

The "Evangelistic Index" was published by the Southern Baptist Convention's Home Mission Board for its internal use. The report as a whole has not been disseminated to the public, but a significant portion was published in the September 5, 1993, issue of the *Birmingham* [Alabama] *News*.

The Southern Baptist Church of Alabama produced the first regional estimates of how many Alabamans are going to hell. They based these on modern data-gathering and statistical methods. But the church did not limit its concern to Alabama. They also calculated how many people from other places are going to hell.

The estimates were a practical tool, a guide for where to concentrate the church's evangelical efforts and where not to bother.

Any well-run modern business does this. A company that sells insurance or cereal or automobiles likes to let its sales force know how many dependable customers are in each region, how many potential new customers, and also how many marginal prospects—people not worth wasting time on. With this information, the sales force can focus its efforts productively. So it is with the Southern Baptist Church of Alabama. Spokesperson Martin King told the *New York Times*:

"If we were selling snow tires, we'd want to ask ourselves, 'Where are the people who need snow tires?' It's kind of a crass analogy, but where are the people who need the Lord? That's where we need to go."

The church assumes that, in a given neighborhood, nearly all the Southern Baptists are already saved (they also assume that, people being people, a certain small percentage are damned idiots). Other Baptist and evangelical denominations are a mixed lot—some are still savable, others have irrevocably blown it. Most, but not all, Catholics are a lost cause. Non-Christians—Jews, Muslims, Hindus, Confucians, atheists, and others who refuse to accept Jesus—can be written off, evangelically speaking.

The Southern Baptist Convention's Home Mission Board did all the work on this. They devised a secret mathematical formula, estimating what percentage of each religious group will go to hell: X% of Southern Baptists, Y% of Episcopalians, Z% of Catholics, and so on. The percentages are based on experience and instinct. The Home Mission Board puts great faith in these estimates.

It was easy to find out how many people of each faith live in each Alabama county. A group called the Glenmary Home Missioners Board, in Ohio, periodically publishes a massive county-by-county survey of the entire US. The Southern Baptist Convention fed the 1990 survey numbers into their secret formula. The result: the "Evangelistic Index," the now-celebrated, county-by-county estimate of how many Alabama residents are, as the professionals put it, "unsaved."

The "Evangelistic Index" was not meant to be celebrated. Like any sales estimate, it was prepared for the organization's internal use only. But someone gave parts of it to Greg Garrison, a reporter for the *Birmingham News*, and the newspaper published a page-one article that began with the news that:

"More than 1.86 million people in Alabama, 46.1% of the state's population, will be damned to Hell if they don't have a born-again experience professing Jesus Christ as their savior, according to a report by Southern Baptist researchers."

The *Birmingham News* mentioned in passing that this was just the half of it—or, to put it more accurately, this was just the one-fiftieth of it:

"The Southern Baptist researchers who compiled the Evangelistic Index did not publicize their estimates for how many Episcopalians, Presbyterians, Lutherans, Methodists, Catholics and others are saved or lost. 'They're not going to reveal the formula,' [spokesman] Steve Cloues said. 'It's just to give you a feel on a state-by-state basis, trying to show there are some areas that the need is more severe than others.'"

Yes, the Southern Baptist Church of Alabama made estimates for how many people are going to hell in every county—not just in the state of Alabama—but in all 50 of the United States of America. The country-wide figures have never been made public, but anyone who needs to know can reconstruct the numbers pretty easily (see box overleaf). And once cracked, the unheavenly secret formula can easily be applied to almost any region of any country on earth.

For mathematically estimating who's going to be hot and who's not, the Southern Baptist Church of Alabama won the 1994 Ig Nobel Prize in the field of Mathematics.

The winners could not, or would not, attend the Ig Nobel Prize Ceremony.

As a tribute to them, the Ig Nobel Board of Governors sent a representative to the little town of Hell, Norway, to interview the local citizenry and solicit their well wishes. The town's highest official, the railroad stationmaster, asked that his congratulations be expressed at the Ig Nobel Prize Ceremony. And so it was that Terje Korsnes, the Norwegian Consul to Boston, appeared at the Ig Nobel Ceremony, saying:

"I was asked to come here tonight and accept custody of this prize on behalf of the people of Hell, Norway. We were delighted to learn that so many people in the great state of Alabama will go to Hell. We have a special place in Hell for all of you."

For a county-by-county estimate of how many Alabama residents are going to hell and to calculate your own chances of going to hell, visit: www.improbablecom/ig/ig-pastwinners.html

MIKHAIL GORBACHEV
IS THE ANTICHRIST

THE OFFICIAL CITATION
THE IG NOBEL MATHMATICS PRIZE WAS
AWARDED TO

Robert W. Faid of Greenville, South Carolina, farsighted and faithful seer of statistics, for calculating the exact odds (710,609,175,188,282,000 to 1) that Mikhail Gorbachev is the Antichrist.

His study was published in the form of a book: *Gorbachev! Has the Real Antichrist Come?* Victory House, 1988.

In 1988, Robert W. Faid solved one of the oldest and most famous problems in mathematics. Yet almost no one noticed. Cracking the nut that was nearly two millennia old, Robert W. Faid calculated the identity of the Antichrist.

In the rarified world of mathematicians, certain problems become the focus of intense debate. The Four-Color Map Problem caused rabid fascination until Wolfgang Haken and Kenneth Appel devised a solution in 1976. Fermat's Last Theorem was all the rage until Andrew Wiles solved it in 1993.

Haken and Appel became instantly famous among mathematicians. Wiles became a worldwide celebrity, his face appearing everywhere in newspapers and on television.

But little public approbation came to Robert W. Faid.

The Antichrist problem has been on the books since about the year 90, when the *Book of John* was published. The book contains four occurrences of the word "Antichrist." John 2:18, for example, says: "Dear children, this is the last hour; and as you have heard that the Antichrist is coming, even now many Antichrists have come. This is how we know it is the last hour."

Over the years, many amateur mathematicians joined the professionals in trying their hand at this delightful, yet maddeningly difficult, puzzle. Eventually it became a favorite old chestnut, something to be wondered at, but perhaps too difficult to ever yield up a solution.

In the 20th century, the problem rose to sudden popularity. In some circles it was now seen to be a fundamental problem of mathematics. Here and there, professional mathematicians hazarded solutions. But their attempts were flawed.

Then, as has happened so often in this rarified branch of science, an amateur stepped in and claimed the glory that had eluded the pros.

Robert W. Faid later wrote that the story "began about 1 A.M. on March 8, 1985, when I was awakened with a tremendous sense that something of great importance was about to happen." Working with almost demonic fury, he elucidated the factors necessary for a solution, reduced them to a set of 11 (or perhaps 22) numbers, and then multiplied everything together. Then glory, hallelujah, there it was. Robert W. Faid had solved the problem. He had calculated the identity of the Antichrist.

In retrospect, it seems almost absurdly simple: the Antichrist is Mikhail Gorbachev, with odds of 710,609,175,188,282,000 to 1.

How did Robert W. Faid do it? He knew that everyone would want to know, so he wrote a book explaining every first and last tittle and jot.

Robert W. Faid is a trained engineer. He is methodical. In the book *Gorbachev! Has the Real Antichrist Come?*, he carefully explains where each number comes from, and where it enters into the calculation. Then he summarizes all the factors. Here is the complete, concise list of the 11 (or perhaps 22) factors:

FEATURE	PROBABILITY	ODDS
1. Mikhail S. Gorbachev in Russian = 666 × 2(+/−3)	95	94
2. Mikhail S. Gorbachev in Russian = 46 × 29 (+/−1)	15	14
3. Mikhail Gorbachev in Russian = 46 × 27 (+/−3)	6	5
4. Mikhail S. Gorbachev in Greek = 888 × 2 (+/−1)	296	295
5. Mikhail S. Gorbachev in Greek = exactly 888	888	887
6. Rise from obscurity over men of equal qualifications	2,000	1,999
7. Soviet population exactly 276 million (Satan's number)	50	49
8. Rules 10 other kingdoms	10	9
9. Exactly 10 kings (Politburo members when elected)	10	9
10. Exactly seven Warsaw Pact nations	10	9
11. Being the eighth "king" or leader of the USSR	8	7

To the nonspecialist—that is, to anyone without Robert W. Faid's education, experience, and understanding, these numbers may be difficult to comprehend. For example, the difference between Robert W. Faid's "Probability" column and his "Odds" column is presumably rather subtle. But multiply the numbers together (see pages 206–8 of *Gorbachev! Has the Real Antichrist Come?* for details), and out pops the final result: 710,609,175,188,282,000.

What does this number mean, this 710,609,175,188,282,000? Robert W. Faid appreciates that many people are intimidated by statistics, and so he explains as simply as he can:

"The calculations indicate that the odds that Gorbachev is the actual and true Antichrist are: 710,609,175,188,282,000 to 1. That means that if you want to bet that Gorbachev is not the true

Antichrist, you will be betting against odds of 710 quadrillion, 609 trillion, 175 billion, 188 million, 282,000.

"To get an idea just how large this number is, let us compare it with the population of the earth today. There are about five billion people living on the earth at this time. The mathematical probability of one person fitting all of the Antichrist prophecy and the hidden clues that we have examined that show that Mikhail S. Gorbachev indeed does fit, is the same as saying that only one person in 359,576,064 earths of the same population as ours would statistically meet them. If we were to assume, and correctly so, that the Antichrist would have to be an adult male, which is about one-fourth of the population, then this number of earths would be four times as many statistically, or 1,438,304,256 with the same population required."

Professional mathematicians find it difficult to argue with the logic of this.

Robert W. Faid's book was published in 1988. It did not receive the attention that its author had a right to expect. Moreover, the book did not come to the attention of certain high-level decision makers who might have made certain decisions differently, had they been aware of the knowledge contained therein. In particular, it probably was not given adequate consideration by the Norwegian Nobel Committee when that august body selected the winners of the 1990 Nobel Prizes.

And thus, it is not wholly inexplicable why in 1990 Mikhail Sergeyevich Gorbachev was awarded the Nobel Peace Prize.

Nor is it wholly inexplicable why in 1993 Robert W. Faid was awarded the Ig Nobel Prize in the field of Mathematics.

The winner could not, or would not, attend the Ig Nobel Prize Ceremony.

He continued his authorial career, producing *Lydia: Seller of Purple* in 1991, *A Scientific Approach to Biblical Mysteries* in 1993, and *A Scientific Approach to More Biblical Mysteries* in 1995.

Jack Van Impe   Rexella Van Impe

The Ig Nobel Prizes

WHAT OTHER EXPERTS SAY

Jack and Rexella Van Impe, themselves Ig Nobel Prize winners (in 2001, for determining that black holes fulfill all of the technical requirements to be the location of hell), produced a 90-minute video called *The Antichrist—Super Deceiver of the New World Order*, which, according to the promotional material, "answers some of the most intriguing questions of this or any other generation." Perhaps the most intriguing of those questions is this one: "What do Kaiser Wilhelm, Benito Mussolini, Adolf Hitler, Joseph Stalin, Nikita Krushchev, John F. Kennedy, Mikhail Gorbachev and Ronald Reagan have in common?" To obtain the answer, you must send $19.95 plus shipping/handling to Jack Van Impe Ministries.

SCENTS AND SENSIBILITY

 Smell is believed to be the most primitive of our senses. This chapter describes two attempts at sophistication.

- The Self-Perfuming Business Suit
- Filter-Equipped Underwear

THE SELF-PERFUMING BUSINESS SUIT

THE OFFICIAL CITATION
THE IG NOBEL ENVIRONMENTAL PROTECTION PRIZE WAS AWARDED TO

Hyuk-ho Kwon of Kolon Company of Seoul, Korea, for inventing the self-perfuming business suit.

When businessmen come home to their wives after a hard night of drinking and smoking for professional purposes, they can, through no fault of their own, look and smell bad. But they don't have to. Hyuk-ho Kwon has made it easy for them to look good and smell good, no matter how late they stay out. Mr. Kwon is the inventor of the self-perfuming business suit.

Hyuk-ho Kwon is an accomplished, yet quietly personable, employee of the Kolon Company. In all of the organization's 21 subsidiaries, which include enterprises ranging from textiles and chemicals to construction, trading, financial services, information processing, and communications, Mr. Kwon is perhaps the only individual who could have perfected this peculiarly stylish technology.

The suits come in pine, lavender, and peppermint. They are impeccably tailored of very fine-quality wool.

The fabric is soaked in microencapsulated scent, and therein lies the delightful rub. Mr. Kwon recommends vigorously rubbing the sleeve whenever a new burst of freshness is wanted. But the wearer seldom needs to make an effort. The scent is always discernable—and especially so whenever the man walks, or moves in any way, because his every slight motion breaks open a few more of the many millions of microscopic scent capsules.

The suits are made to keep their character through 20 or more dry cleanings—an estimated two to three years of typical use.

Kolon has two major competitors in the self-perfuming-business-suit market—L.G. Fashion, and Essess Heartist. All of them are based in Korea. The Korean fashion industry has transformed itself from a staid manufacturer of foreign designs into an aggressive innovator. When the self-perfuming-business-suit market has established itself throughout the rest of Asia and on the other continents, the newest of the new will still, fashion analysts expect, be coming from Seoul.

Even in its earliest days, the self-perfuming-business-suit market was not limited to married executives. Single, young executives-of-the-future also recognized the sweet smell of success.

"My lavender [scented] suit helps me keep the peace at home," office worker Lee Gyung-wook told Reuters news agency, echoing countless of his married, self-perfuming-business-suited superiors. "Without it, my parents would be all over me because of the stench of *soju* [Korean liquor] and spicy side dishes after nights out with my colleagues and friends," Lee said. "It's a huge relief since I no longer have to pour cheap cologne all over me. All I have to do now is just shake and shimmy in front of my house, and then go in with a frown on my face, saying, 'Man, I hate night shifts.'" Reuters also interviewed Moon Chol-ho, 28, who said: "After a hard day's work, we don't smell good with sweat. It's nice to wear the scented suit. It doesn't give off an unpleasant smell to others."

For engineering fail-safe fragrances into the traditional business suit, Hyuk-ho Kwon won the 1999 Ig Nobel Prize in the field of Environmental Protection.

Mr. Kwon traveled from Seoul, Korea, at his company's expense, to attend the Ig Nobel Prize Ceremony. The Kolon Company generously made self-perfuming business suits for the five Nobel Laureates who participated in the ceremony, and for the master of ceremonies. Self-scented business suits dominated Sanders Theatre. In accepting his Ig Nobel Prize, Mr. Kwon said:

"Thank you. The stronger you rub it, the stronger it smells. Thank you. It's my greatest pleasure to have the honor of receiving this prize. I just put my faith in God, hoping that there will be fragrance in my life. However, I came to realize that fragrance is in my suit. So, since I expect my lifetime to be fragrant, I hope every one of you may have fragrance in your life."

FILTER-EQUIPPED UNDERWEAR

THE OFFICIAL CITATION
THE IG NOBEL BIOLOGY PRIZE WAS AWARDED TO

Buck Weimer of Pueblo, Colorado, for inventing Under-Ease, airtight underwear with a replaceable charcoal filter that removes bad-smelling gases before they escape.

Under-Ease is described in US Patent # 5,593,398 ("Protective Underwear with Malodorous Flatus Filter"). The product is available in men's and women's models from Under-Tec Corporation of Pueblo, Colorado (telephone 888-433-5913 in the US, 719-584-7782 outside the US), www.under-tec.com.

After years of olfactory suffering, Buck Weimer chose to invent a solution to his wife's intermittent, explosive problem. Unembarrassed, the couple was then kind enough to share that solution with the world.

A June 2001 report in the *Denver* [Colorado] *Post* told the story clearly:

"Buck Weimer, 62, of Pueblo, [tells] what happened after a huge Thanksgiving dinner more than six years ago. He and his wife, Arlene, 57, who suffers from Crohn's disease, a form of inflammatory bowel syndrome, were lying under the covers when she let go a bomb.

" 'I'm lying in bed with her, sort of suffering silently,' he said. 'Out of the silence came determination. Something had to be done.' More than six years later, Buck Weimer has a new invention: Under-Ease, airtight underwear with a replaceable charcoal filter that removes bad-smelling gases before they escape. Weimer received a patent in 1998.

"The undies are made from a soft, airtight, nylon-type fabric. Elastic is sewn around the waist and both legs. The removable filter—which looks similar to the shoulder pads placed in women's clothing—is made of charcoal sandwiched between two layers of Australian sheep's wool."

Weimer began the research and development process by trying to modify a standard gas mask. When that proved unsuitable to the task, he began tinkering. The final design is a slick, low-tech device.

Biologists love hearing Weimer describe the action of the filter mechanism:

"The multilayered filter pad traps the 1–2% of human gas creat-

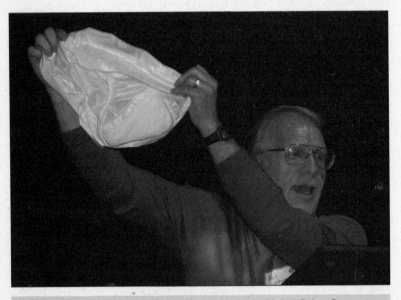

Buck Weimer and a pair of Under-Ease at the Ig Nobel Prize Ceremony. Photo: Jon Chase/Harvard News Office.

ing the foul smell (mostly hydrogen sulfide), but allows the remaining nonsmelling gas (mostly methane) to pass through. It also allows the natural buildup of body heat to pass through."

Engineers love hearing how it is constructed:

"A triangular 'exit hole' for the flatus to be expelled is cut from the back of the airtight underwear, near the bottom. This 'exit hole' is covered with a 'pocket' made of ordinary porous fabric sewn over the 'exit hole.' This unique design forces all expelled gas (flatus) out through the 'pocket.'"

Business gurus love hearing the company's motto: "Wear them for the ones you love."

Under-Ease comes in boxers for men, and panties for women. Replacement filters are available at low cost.

For easing the biological and social interactions of his fellow human beings, Buck Weimer won the 2001 Ig Nobel Prize in the field of Biology.

The winner and his wife traveled from Colorado, at their own expense, to attend the Ig Nobel Prize Ceremony. Buck Weimer presented pairs of Under-Ease to the Nobel Laureates, and instructed them on how to use it. In accepting the Prize, he said:

"My acceptance speech comes in the shape of a song. I think you all may remember it. It's called 'Imagine.'"

> Imagine no odorous gas.
> It's easy if you try:
> No more burning nostrils,
> Our tush securely covered.
> Imagine all the people
> Wearing Under-Ease.
>
> You might say I'm a dreamer.
> But I'm not the only one.
> My wife is here also.
> I hope someday you'll join us
> With Under-Ease
> the world will be one.

Imagine the odorless sound—
I wonder if you can.
No need for divorce or separation.
Free from shame and guilt.
Imagine all the people
sharing Under-Ease.

I'm almost finished . . .

You may say I'm a dreamer,
but I'm not the only one.
My wife is still here.
I hope someday you'll join us,
with Under-Ease
the world will live as one.

FOOD FOR THOUGHT

 Some people live to eat, some eat to live, and others do something else entirely. Here are seven examples:

- Extremely Instant Barbeque
- Sogginess at Breakfast
- The Effects of Ale, Garlic, and Soured Cream on the Appetite of Leeches
- No Need for Food
- How to Make a Cup of Tea, Officially
- The Sociology of Canadian Donut Shops
- The Optimal Way to Dunk a Biscuit

Extremely Instant Barbecue

THE OFFICIAL CITATION

THE IG NOBEL CHEMISTRY PRIZE WAS AWARDED TO

George Goble of Purdue University, for his blistering world record time for igniting a barbecue grill—three seconds—using charcoal and liquid oxygen.

George Goble's Web site (*http://ghg.ecn.purdue.edu/~ghg*) features video of a quick grill ignition.

A computer engineer at Purdue University decided to optimize the process of igniting a barbecue grill. He succeeded.

George Goble likes barbecues. That is why he destroys them. The destruction is a mere side effect. The point of it all is speed.

The history of the project, like the ignition, is enlightening and brief. Goble once explained it to a local newspaper:

"Goble said he got the idea after cooking out with engineer pals for several years. 'It always took a half-hour to 40 minutes to get the thing going, so we started using hairdryers, a vacuum on low, and propane torches to get it going,' Goble said. 'Then we took an oxygen tank like the kind scuba divers use and blew it through a ten-foot-long pipe. We were grilling in 30 seconds. Every year we got it started faster and faster until we got it down to a few seconds with so much pressure that it blew the briquettes out of the grill.'"

The optimized procedure is simplicity itself. Goble asks someone

George Goble ignites his lunch. Photo: Joe Cychosz.

to throw a lighted cigarette onto the grill. Then he pours three gallons of liquid oxygen onto the cigarette.

Safety is the number one, or, at worst, number two, concern. Goble pours the liquid oxygen from an eight-foot-long wooden pole. Spectators are kept at an almost reasonable distance. "Don't stare at the flame unless you squint," he advises them. "It's like the sun."

While a cheap grill is entirely consumed by the fire, a sturdy make—a good Weber grill, for example, can survive two to three liquid oxygen barbecues before all trace of it vanishes.

Having achieved a consistent sub-four-second ignition time, and having attracted increasingly annoyed complaints from local fire officials, Goble has publicly stated that, in future, if he prepares ultra-fast food, it will not be in this particular manner.

For establishing a new standard for barbecue grill ignition, George Goble won the 1996 Ig Nobel Prize in the field of Chemistry.

The winner could not travel to the Ig Nobel Prize Ceremony, but instead sent his colleague Joe Cychosz to accept on his behalf. Mr. Cychosz (who pronounces his name, with lifelong matter-of-factness, like the plural of "the word psycho") said:

"It's hard to believe all that work started back with a hairdryer and a bunch of people who wanted to eat real quick. On behalf of George, I'd like to thank the Board of Governors."

Sogginess at Breakfast

THE OFFICIAL CITATION
THE IG NOBEL PHYSICS PRIZE WAS AWARDED TO

D.M.R. Georget, R. Parker, and A.C. Smith of the Institute of Food Research, Norwich, England, for their rigorous analysis of soggy breakfast cereal, published in the report, "A Study of the Effects of Water Content on the Compaction Behaviour of Breakfast Cereal Flakes."

Their study was published in *Powder Technology*, November 1994, vol. 81, no. 2, pp. 189–96.

Many people, of a morning, wonder why their breakfast cereal becomes soggy. Thanks to a painstaking investigation conducted in 1994, the answer is now on the public record.

D.M.R. Georget, Roger Parker, and Andrew Smith looked at the basic physics of a breakfast cereal flake.

They examined the flake with fresh eyes, augmented by the obvious battery of equipment: a Mettler LP16 moisture balance; an Instron 1122 Universal testing machine; a piston-driven capillary rheometer; and all the rest.

Prior to this time, anyone who wanted to understand the basic physics of a breakfast cereal flake had to camp out in engineering libraries and dig through the many reports that touched on this or that aspect of breakfast-cereal-flake behavior.

Georget, Parker, and Smith did things methodically. Before

touching their cereal, the three chums devoured the published works of all the great breakfast-cereal-flake researcher teams: Peleg, Kawakita and Heckel; Roberts and Rowe; Train and York; Illka and Paronen; and the never-to-be-forgotten Marousis and Saravacos.

Once they knew what was known and what was not, Georget, Parker, and Smith got right down to business. They obtained breakfast cereal flakes. They performed experiments. They did calculations. They plotted plots and graphed graphs. And ultimately, they solved the puzzle.

Basically, they soaked some flakes in water, then dropped them into a cylinder, and then stuck a thingy down into the cylinder to compress the flakes. They measured how much the flakes compressed as they got soggier and soggier. To get a thorough picture of the sogging process, they did this again and again, each time using slightly soggier flakes.

They discovered that, up to a point, as a flake takes on liquid, it retains much of its girlish firmness. But after that point, it goes suddenly limp. To put this in simple language: the Heckel deformation stress becomes increasingly sensitive to the particle density as the water content increased. That may seem obvious now, but at the time it was only fairly obvious.

The journey from crisp to soggy is considerably more colorful than people expect, especially in a numerical sense. For example: the biggest changes in sogginess come as the water content of the flake increases from 12% to 18%. But the fun is in crunching all the numbers, so the reader is urged to get a copy of Georget, Parker, and Smith's full report, and also perhaps get a bowl of cereal, and sit down for a multidimensional, crackling good feast of the senses.

A word of caution, though—Georget, Parker, and Smith obtained all their results using water. In theory, their results will hold up when, some day, someone repeats the experiments using milk. For the time being, the story seems to hold water.

Georget, Parker, and Smith's "Study of the Effects of Water Content on the Compaction Behaviour of Breakfast Cereal Flakes" is a high point in the intellectual history of cereal-flake soggification. For advancing our basic understanding of what happens in the bowl,

D.M.R. Georget, Roger Parker, and Andrew Smith won the 1995 Ig Nobel Prize in the field of Physics.

The winners could not travel to the Ig Nobel Prize Ceremony. Instead they sent a videotaped acceptance speech of themselves in their lab, with a bowl of cereal. In the video, Andrew Smith spoke for the three of them:

"In our study of compaction of breakfast cereal flakes, we did not leave them turned tongue-in-cheek, or use any other sensory technique. Rather, we set out to relate macroscale mechanical properties to changes in the scale of constituent food particle molecules. This provides valuable insights into texture. So what does this mean for the manufacturer, and to you, the consumer? Well, it's all about the quest for the ultimate breakfast-cereal-eating experience. I hope that the awarding of this Prize will stimulate further research in this area."

Note: news of this particular Prize indirectly touched off the curious affair of the chief scientific adviser's Angry Complaint. See the introductory section of this book for details.

THE EFFECTS OF ALE, GARLIC, AND SOURED CREAM ON THE APPETITE OF LEECHES

THE OFFICIAL CITATION
THE IG NOBEL BIOLOGY PRIZE WAS AWARDED TO

Anders Baerheim and Hogne Sandvik of the University of Bergen, Norway, for their tasty and tasteful report, "Effect of Ale, Garlic, and Soured Cream on the Appetite of Leeches."

Their study was published in the *British Medical Journal*, vol. 309, December 24–31, 1994, p. 1689.

How, exactly, does one stimulate the appetite of a leech?

Until the mid-20th century, leeches were a common tool in medicine. Recently, after several generations of disuse, they have made a rather glamorous return to the medical scene. Surgeons who perform certain kinds of microsurgery clamor for leeches. In reattaching a severed finger, for example, it is crucial to keep the blood from clotting—and applying a leech is far and away the best known way to do that.

A hungry leech is a welcome addition to a surgical team. Yet leeches, like most humans, are not reliable trenchermen. And in a surgical emergency, a sated, passive leech is of no use.

Then how does one stimulate the appetite of a leech? Chances are your doctor would rely on the wisdom passed down from medical authorities of the 19th and early 20th centuries: that beer or soured cream are guaranteed to give even the most bloated leech a powerful case of the munchies.

Until quite recently, medicine was very much an art, and almost not at all a science. In 1994, Anders Baerheim and Hogne Sandvik realized that no one had scientifically tested the conventional methods of leech appetite stimulation. This, therefore, was what they set out to do. And, in addition to testing the traditional leech treats—beer and soured cream—they added a new delight: garlic.

Baerheim and Sandvik used a simple laboratory procedure:

"Six leeches were dipped briefly in one of two different types of beer (Guinness stout or Hansa bock) ... before being placed on the forearm of one of us (HS). We measured the time from when the leech touched the skin until HS felt it bite. Each leech was exposed three times to each liquid in random order."

The experiment yielded clear results:

Beer: "After exposure to beer, some of the leeches changed behavior, swaying their forebodies, losing grip, or falling on their backs."

Garlic: "Two leeches placed on the forearm smeared with garlic started to wriggle and crawl without assuming the sucking position ... Their condition deteriorated. When placed on a bare arm they tried to initiate feeding but did not manage to coordinate the process. Both died 2½ hours after the exposure to garlic. For ethical reasons the garlic arm was abandoned at this point."

Soured cream: "Leeches exposed to soured cream became ravenous. When they were then placed into a glass beaker, they 'sucked frantically on the wall of their container after they had been on the arm.' While they were still on the arm, however, they bit no sooner than leeches that had been deprived of sour cream or any other artificial stimulant."

So, how does one stimulate the appetite of a leech? Science does not really know. But best not with beer or garlic, and likely not with soured cream.

Anders Baerheim and Hogne Sandvik scientifically—and boldly—tested the medical profession's best accepted "wisdom." They demonstrated that the conventional wisdom was wrong. For this they were awarded the 1996 Ig Nobel Prize in the field of Biology.

The winners could not attend the Ig Nobel Prize Ceremony, but instead sent a videotaped acceptance speech:

"We accept this Prize with profound gratitude. We accept it as a tribute to our partners, the leeches, who showed remarkable enthusi-asm during our experiments. Lab animals seldom receive credit for their scientific achievements. The leeches' reaction to this honor was predictable—they celebrated. Since the leeches are in no fit state to accept this award today, we have to rely on a stand-in. As he is not a leech, we are confident he will behave with proper dignity."

The mysterious "stand-in" turned out to be a tall, somber-faced gentleman named Terje Korsnes, Norway's honorary consul to Mass-achusetts. Korsnes stepped to the lectern, delivered a brief speech to the 1,200 people in the packed theater, and then he delivered some-thing else. What he said was:

"Thank you. My countrymen Baerheim and Sandvik couldn't physically make it to the ceremony. Clearly, this kind of break-through research should be recognized. I'm sure that this is the kind of recognition that the scientific community in Bergen has been waiting for. I do fear that this topic is not taken seriously here in Cambridge. Perhaps in this audience with bright minds there is

The Ig Nobel Prizes

NOT ALL SCIENTISTS ARE SHY

Anders Baerheim and Hogne Sandvik are unique in the ranks of Ig Nobel Prize winners.

After publishing "Effect of Ale, Garlic, and Soured Cream on the Appetite of Leeches" in the prestigious *British Medical Journal*, they sent a copy of it to the Ig Nobel Board of Gover-nors, accompanied by a note explaining why they believed themselves deserving of an Ig Nobel Prize.

In 1996, they were selected to win one of that year's crop of Igs. They triumphed against a field of several thousand nom-inees, several hundred of whom had nominated themselves.

Although every year many people nominate themselves for an Ig Nobel Prize, of the more than 100 Prizes awarded so far, the team of Baerheim and Sandvik is the only self-nominated winner.

someone who would like to leech onto this topic for further research. To facilitate that, I have brought these leeches to distribute among you so you can start your project."

At that point he reached into his suit pocket, removed a bagful of leeches, and began throwing them into the audience. The leeches were made of plastic, but the Ig Nobel organizers had no way of knowing that—and the audience *certainly* had no way of knowing it.

And so, on that day, the world learned something about leeches and about medicine, and it also learned something about Norwegian diplomats.

No Need for Food

THE OFFICIAL CITATION
THE IG NOBEL LITERATURE PRIZE WAS AWARDED TO

Jasmuheen (formerly known as Ellen Greve) of Australia, first lady of Breatharianism, for her book *Living on Light*, which explains that, although some people do eat food, they don't ever really need to.

Jasmuheen described her nutritional history and outlook in the book *Living on Light*, KOHA Publishing, 1998.

The Breatharians are a loose-knit, but jolly, group who say they enjoy not eating together, and also enjoy not eating alone. The basic fact of Breatharianism is that they say they don't eat at all: and if they do eat, it is for social reasons or for entertainment, not for nourishment.

Jasmuheen, whose original name is Ellen Greve, says that she last ate a proper meal in 1993. Her sustenance and vitality since that time has come from "tapping into an alternative source of nourishment." Her diligence and lack of diet have made her the best-known Breatharian.

What is Breatharianism? To those who attend her seminars or buy her books, Jasmuheen offers a clear, simple definition of the practice:

"Breatharianism is the ability to absorb all the nutrients, vitamins, and nourishment one requires, to maintain a healthy physical vehicle, from the universal life force, or chi energy. A being who practices this does not need to eat food."

Jasmuheen practices this, and does not need to eat food. As reported on the back cover of her bestselling book *Living on Light*, "Since 1993, Jasmuheen has been physically nourished by the Universal Life Force of Prana."

Despite her obvious glowing good health and high spirits, Jasmuheen has been afflicted by quibblers and doubters. A report in *The Times* of London, on April 6, 2000, for example, said that an Australian journalist who was checking on to a flight with Jasmuheen was surprised to hear the airline attendant ask the cult leader to confirm that she had ordered a vegetarian meal. Jasmuheen quickly denied it, then changed her mind. " 'Yes, I did, but I won't be eating it,' she said."

Jasmuheen is gracious in dealing with skeptics. On her Web site she addressed this very incident:

"Fact: a *Daily Mirror* reporter overheard a flight-check-in lady confirming a 10-year standing note on my ticket for vegetarian food that I have never bothered to change. Fact: on long flights I sometimes eat a potato to send me to sleep as when I never eat I find it very hard to sleep. Eating a small amount can activate the digestive process, drops our energy levels, and lets us sleep. No big deal."

The year before, the Australian news program *60 Minutes* arranged a test of Jasmuheen's claims. They sealed her into a hotel room in Brisbane for seven days, with a team of reporters watching closely to see that she ingested no food, and a doctor on hand to monitor her health. On the third day, the doctor expressed concern that she was showing signs of dehydration and physical distress, and so Jasmuheen and the entire group moved to a pleasant, and presumably less stressful, mountain retreat just outside the city. Two days later, *60 Minutes* halted the test and rushed Jasmuheen to a hospital.

In this case, Jasmuheen answered the critics, as she always does, with her trademark tact and honesty. Her organization issued a press release saying:

"*60 Minutes* decided to not continue the Challenge with Jasmuheen as she entered day 5 of the 7 days, on the advice of the attending Doctor, Dr. Wenck. As Dr. Wenck had not read Jasmuheen's in-depth research into this matter, the doctor became most concerned by Jasmuheen's weight loss and slight dehydration as would any doctor who was unfamiliar with the last 7 years of research into this matter. As Jasmuheen told *60 Minutes* before they began, it was imperative that they read the book detailing her research on this, so that they could be well informed as to the changes that would occur within Jasmuheen's system and not panic. Despite this, the producer, Richard Carleton, and Dr. Wenck admitted to Jasmuheen that they had not read this literature and hence, when they found themselves in what they felt was a potentially dangerous situation, they pulled the plug even though Jasmuheen was happy and able to safely continue."

Despite the doubters and the cynics, Jasmuheen has prospered. Her organization, the Cosmic Internet Academy, which is also known as the CIA, and which is dedicated to One People in Harmony to the Planet, distributes educational materials and arranges seminars and retreats. Reportedly, her books (*Pranic Nourishment, In Resonance, Inspirations* (Volumes I, II, & III), *Streams of Consciousness* (Volumes 1, 2, & 3), *Our Camelot—the Game of DA, Ambassadors of Light, Living on Light, Our Progeny—the X-re-Generation,* and *Dancing with My DOW)* and tapes *(Australia Overseas, Breath of Life, Inner Sanctuary, Emotional Realignment, Meditation for Empowerment, Ascension Acceleration, Self-Healing Meditation,* and *Akashic Records Meditation*), her five-day Luscious Lifestyles Retreats, and her seven-day MAPS (Movement of an Awakened Positive Society) International Retreats all sell well, requiring her to keep a busy international schedule.

People constantly ask Jasmuheen whether she lost weight after giving up food. The answer is yes: "I programmed my body to reach a certain weight and stabilize there. I maintained a weight of 47–48 kilos (104–106 lbs) from that time regardless of how much fluid I drank or how many intermittent mouthfuls of flavor I experimented with."

She goes on to explain that "Trying to gain weight after the process is more difficult than simply addressing the underlying belief patterns and not losing it in the first place!" One year, despite the tremendous difficulty, she did manage to gain eight kilos (18 lbs).

Although Breatharians can achieve nearly complete control over all bodily functions, Jasmuheen counsels that sometimes there are social reasons to do otherwise. For example, "Regarding menstruation, as I have completed my childbearing, I thought it would be convenient to program for the body to cease bleeding. When this did not work I asked the Masters for guidance and was told that regular menstruation was a 'traditionally' acceptable sign of a healthy body and it was, and would be, important to continue to display signs of complete health."

On Jasmuheen's Web site (*www.jasmuheen.com*) she says that her top priority is "to healthily feed, clothe, comfortably shelter and holistically educate the earth's people by 2012."

For her efforts to feed things to the world, Jasmuheen won the 2000 Ig Nobel Prize in the field of Literature.

The winner could not, or would not, attend the Ig Nobel Prize Ceremony, but did carry on an engaging E-mail conversation with the Ig Nobel Board of Governors. The discussion was wide-ranging, not so much in topic as in location. Jasmuheen was traveling from country to country, conducting seminars and sampling the local light. She expressed pride and delight at winning the Ig Nobel Prize, and regret at having previously scheduled a very lucrative event in Brazil that would preclude her coming to Harvard.

How to Make a Cup of Tea, Officially

THE OFFICIAL CITATION
THE IG NOBEL PRIZE IN LITERATURE WAS AWARDED TO
The British Standards Institution, for its six-page specification (BS 6008) of the proper way to make a cup of tea.

What is the proper way to make a cup of tea? The question has many answers, but only one of them is the official British Standard.

The Tea Standard was issued by the British Standards Institution, an organization known, as affectionately as a standards institution can be known, as "the BSI."

As with all standards promulgated by the BSI, the Tea Standard has a formal name, and it has a number. "Method for Preparation of a Liquor of Tea for Use in Sensory Tests" is standard number BS 6008.

BS 6008 has stood unchanged since 1980. In printed form it is six pages long, and it is valuable. The exact value is £20, the per-copy price at which it is sold by the British Standards Institution.

To those not steeped in the tea trade, the word "liquor" in the title may be confusing. The BSI points out that in this usage "liquor has no attachments to alcohol or spirits," instead meaning "a solution prepared by extraction of soluble substances."

What does it mean to make a cup of tea? Officially, it means to take "extraction of soluble substances in dried tea leaf, contained in a porcelain or earthenware pot, by means of freshly boiling water, pouring of the liquor into a white porcelain or earthenware bowl." The pot must have "its edge partly serrated and provided with a lid, the skirt of which fits loosely inside the pot."

BS 6008 is flexible. It includes provisions for making tea with milk ("pour milk free from any off-flavour into the bowl") or without.

Here is a much-abridged version of the British Tea Standard, BS 6008:

- Use 2 g ($^1/_{16}$ oz) of tea—plus or minus 2%—for every 100 ml ($^1/_2$ cup) of water.
- Tea flavour and appearance will be affected by the hardness of the water used.
- Fill the pot to within 4–6 mm ($^1/_5$ inch) of the brim with freshly boiling water.
- After the lid has been placed on top, leave the pot to brew for precisely six minutes.
- Add milk at a ratio of 1.75 ml ($^1/_{128}$ cup) of milk for every 100 ml ($^1/_2$ cup) of tea.
- Lift the pot with the lid in place, then "pour tea through the infused leaves into the cup."
- Pour in tea on top of milk to prevent scalding the milk. If you pour your milk in last, the best results are with a liquor temperature of 65–80 degrees C (150–175°F).

Altogether the British Standards Institution publishes more than 15,000 standards covering seemingly all aspects of commercial and daily life. Numerically, the Tea Standard comes just after BS 6007 ("Rubber-Insulated Cables for Electric Power and Lighting") and right before BS 6009 ("Hypodermic Needles for Single Use: Colour Coding for Identification"). Other favorites from the 6000 series include:

BS 6094–"Methods for Laboratory Beating of Pulp"
BS 6102–"Screw Threads Used to Assemble Head Fittings on Bicycle Forks"
BS 6271–"Miniature Hacksaw Blades"

The **Ig Nobel Prizes**

PROFESSOR LIPSCOMB MAKES A CUP OF TEA

Among the Nobel Laureates participating in the 1999 Ig Nobel Prize Ceremony, one was so moved by the British Tea Standard that he presented BSI representative Reginald Blake with an additional, personal tribute. For the benefit of Mr. Blake and the suddenly tea-crazed 1,200 audience members, William Lipscomb, the 1976 Nobel Chemistry Prize winner, showed and narrated a slide show called *Professor Lipscomb Makes a Cup of Tea*. The two images reproduced here give a glimpse of how the Harvard chemistry professor scientifically prepares his favorite beverage.

BS 6310—"Occluded-Ear Simulator for the Measurement of Ear-phones Coupled to the Ear by Ear Inserts"

BS 6366—"Studs for Rugby Football Boots"

BS 6386—"Tool Chucks with Clamp Screws for Flatted Parallel Shanks: Dimensions of Chuck Nose"

To many literary critics, these other standards do not approach the aesthetic heights reached by BS 6008, "Method for Preparation of a Liquor of Tea for Use in Sensory Tests." The hot, steamy prose of BS 6008 epitomizes literature, propriety, and tea time, setting a standard to which all can sippingly adhere.

For their six-page classic, the British Standards Institution was awarded the 1999 Ig Nobel Prize in the field of Literature.

A representative of the British Standards Institution traveled, at the BSI's expense, from England to the Ig Nobel Prize Ceremony. Wearing a dark business suit, a top hat surmounted with a small

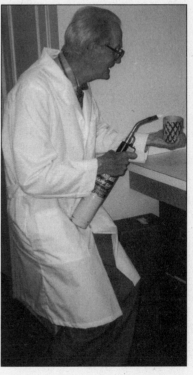

Highlights from the slide show *Professor Lipscomb Makes a Cup of Tea*, Nobel Laureate William Lipscomb's personal tribute to the winner of the 1999 Ig Nobel Literature Prize. *Left*: Professor Lipscomb obtains water. *Right*: Professor Lipscomb puts it to the boil.

teapot, and teacups dangling over his ears, Reginald Blake arrived at the airport in Boston and took the short cab ride to the ceremony at Harvard University. With every fiber of his very proper being, Mr. Blake strained to make clear that he was representing not just his employer, but also the entire British tradition of making and drinking tea. He said:

"It has only taken us 5,000 years to develop a standard on how to make hot tea, so don't expect to see a cold-tea or an iced-tea one until the year 7000. By the way, we Brits have concluded that the Boston Tea Party was simply the first attempt to make iced tea on a grand scale. How do you make a cup of tea very quickly: you put 2 g mass of tea per 100 ml of water. I'm not going to do the conversion for you. Fill the pots within 4–6 mm of the brim, and put on the lid. Brew for six minutes. Pour 5 ml of milk into a cup and pour in the tea. In the best traditions, I'd like to thank BSI, the Boston Philharmonic, and Julius Caesar of 'I came, I saw, I had a cup of tea' fame. Thank you."

The audience pelted Mr. Blake with paper airplanes, tea bags, and affection.

THE SOCIOLOGY OF CANADIAN DONUT SHOPS

THE OFFICIAL CITATION
THE IG NOBEL SOCIOLOGY PRIZE WAS AWARDED TO

Steve Penfold, of York University in Toronto, for doing his Ph.D. thesis on the sociology of Canadian donut shops.

His Ph.D. thesis, prepared for the history department at York University, is titled "The Social Life of Donuts: Commodity and Community in the Golden Horseshoe, 1950–1999." A preliminary essay version was published as "'Eddie Shack Was No Tim Horton': Donuts and the Folklore of Mass Culture in Canada," in the book *Food Nations: Selling Taste in Consumer Societies,* Warren Belasco and Philip Scranton, editors, Routledge, 2001, pp. 48–66.

As a graduate student in the history department of York University, Steve Penfold had to choose a topic that required original research on a subject of interest to scholars in his field. Penfold chose to write about the place of donut shops in the social fabric of Canada.

Canadians eat more donuts per capita than any other people on earth. The largest share of those donuts is obtained from and/or eaten at the almost 2,000 Tim Horton's donut shops spread across Canada. These shops, named after a professional hockey player now deceased, out-number McDonald's restaurants. For many Canadians, and for many Canadian towns, the Tim Horton's, with its donuts, its coffee, and its well-heated place of shelter from the winter that dominates the Canadian psyche, is the key to social life. Penfold explained to the *Wall Street Journal* that "In England, people go to the local pub to socialize; in Canada, they go to the local donut shop."

Here are some extracts from his work.

"In Canada, the donut is widely believed to be the unofficial national food. Indeed, the fatty treat is celebrated as a sort of ironic replacement for the dramatic national symbols found south of the 49th parallel. We consume American products, yet somehow crave a more 'genuine' Canadian mass culture experience, like a Tim Horton's coffee on a February morning. Expatriate Canadians speak of associating a trip to the donut shop with returning home.

"The rise of these national associations seems curiously disconnected from the origins and the fate of the commodity itself. As with much of 20th-century Canadian economic history, big-time donut retailers developed in Canada as branch plants or Canadian-owned versions of US mass-production ideas. In 1995, Tim Horton's was sold to Wendy's. While Canadians are normally sensitive to the threat of American-owned companies, the sale of this 'national institution' to an American hamburger company did not seem to affect Tim Horton's link to national mythology.

"If we believe that the dynamic of mass culture is to degrade production on the one hand and to reduce social experience to consumption on the other, then the donut takes on considerable analytic power. In Canada, the donut is mainly produced by large companies, sold in cookie-cutter shops across the country, and served by low-wage workers doing carefully defined, unskilled jobs. Yet the donut is also a vehicle for ironic depictions of Canadian life. Ultimately, the effect of donut folklore—the nature of its mediation of structure and identity, of mass and community—remains ambiguous."

For finding new meaning in donuts, Steve Penfold won the 1999 Ig Nobel Prize in the field of Sociology.

The winner traveled to the Ig Nobel Prize Ceremony, at his own expense. In accepting the Prize, he said:

"Well, I understand that in America, doing a Ph.D. thesis on the sociology and the history of donut shops might be considered a little off. I don't know. In Canada, this is considered quite normal. In fact, quite noble, if I may use that word. In fact, people come up to me in the street and say, 'Way to go, buddy. Good job, eh.' Because you may not realize the donut is Canada's national food. Poems are written in tribute. Songs sing the praises of our fatty treat. Yet, as a Canadian, I am proud to say that to get this award in the city that originated the chain donut store, Boston, Massachusetts, indeed, you are so well supplied with donuts, I would move here if it weren't for only one problem: as I walk around, there's too many Americans! A whole city filled with Americans. And I have no problem with that, you being Americans in the privacy of your own home, but don't do it on the street where everybody else can see."

Writing a doctoral thesis on the sociology of Canadian donut shops is not the least stressful of all possible experiences. In a departmental newsletter in 2001, one of Steve Penfold's fellow graduate students touched on this:

"I went to a session on tips and strategies for thesis writers. Did I learn anything? Well, yes. Steve Penfold, probably unwittingly, taught me a lesson. On that day, I heard Steve—the donut man, for those of you don't know him by his real name—ask twice how not to kill everybody around him while writing his thesis. During the session, when the question came up again, I could not help but to worry about his state of mind which obviously originated from the fact that he has been working on his thesis . . . for too long? Steve's aggressiveness plunged me into deep thoughts about my work and mostly about my life outside academia . . . I remain hopeful that Steve Penfold will only stay famous for his passion for donuts and not because of some horrific event involving the killing of his family."

THE OPTIMAL WAY TO
DUNK A BISCUIT

THE OFFICIAL CITATION
THE IG NOBEL PHYSICS PRIZE WAS AWARDED TO
Dr. Len Fisher of Bath, England, and Sydney, Australia, for calculating the optimal way to dunk a biscuit
... and ...
Professor Jean-Marc Vanden-Broeck of the University of East Anglia, England, and Belgium, for calculating how to make a teapot spout that does not drip.

To dunk a biscuit, to pour tea from a pot—these are activities of joy and grace, exemplars of the art of living. And, like everything else in the universe, they are ripe for scientific analysis. Two men of great learning and tenacity, working independently and thirsting for knowledge and tea, drew out nature's secret recipes for how to dunk and how to pour.

Len Fisher was the first person to recognize, or at least the first person to bother to recognize, that dunking a biscuit makes more sense if you use a belt sander, an X-ray machine, scales, and a microscope, and apply the Washburn equation for capillary flow in a porous material, and if you are a physicist, which he is.

Happily for the biscuit-dunking public, Dr. Fisher took the time (aided by research funding from McVitie's) to translate the technicalities so they would be palatable to the average dip-and-munch Joe in the street. He produced a simpler version of the equation, and also some guidelines:

- Different biscuits have different optimal dunking times (a gingernut biscuit reaches its dunkability zenith at approximately three seconds, a digestive biscuit at eight seconds).
- Biscuits with chocolate on one side are optimally dipped biscuit-side down; or failing that, at an angle.

Being a scientist, Dr. Fisher also produced a nice set of numbers and charts.

Meanwhile, in Norwich, a mathematician named Jean-Marc Vanden-Broeck was reaching the climax of a 17-year-long effort to design, at least theoretically, a nondripping teapot spout. A professor at the University of East Anglia, the Belgian native is an expert in the difficult field of fluid dynamics.

Why the magnificent obsession with teapots? Partly it's because this really does constitute a very interesting and difficult problem in the physicomathematics of fluids and surfaces. Though it gets little public acclaim, there is a rich history of scientific inquiry into how things drip. [The interested reader is urged to delve into the prestigious physics research journal *Physical Review Letters*, which in recent years has published papers titled "Theoretical Analysis of a Dripping Faucet" (2000), "Suppression of Dripping from a Ceiling" (2001), and the provocative "Dripping Faucet with Ants" (1998).]

But there may be another reason. Mathematicians—good ones, anyway—are much in demand to give talks at universities around the world. Almost inevitably, an academic talk is preceded by tea. After getting dripped upon one too many times, a scientist with pertinent expertise and experience could very well let annoyance become a spur to his keen imagination.

Especially after he discovered the secret to a dripless teapot, Professor Vanden-Broeck was being invited to figure in events such as this one advertised for June 1, 2001, at the University of Edinburgh:

> ## SEMINAR
>
> ## JEAN-MARC VANDEN-BROECK (UEA)
>
> Seminars Take Place at 3:30 P.M. Everybody is Welcome.
> TEA IS SERVED AT 3 P.M. IN THE COMMON ROOM.

Similarly, Dr. Len Fisher, discoverer of the optimal way to dunk a biscuit, became a popular figure on the scientific tea-and-biscuits scene.

For their scientific discoveries with teapots and biscuits, Jean-Marc Vanden-Broeck and Len Fisher shared the 1999 Ig Nobel Prize in the field of Physics.

Professor Vanden-Broeck could not, or would not, attend the Ig Nobel Prize Ceremony, but Dr. Fisher traveled from Bristol, England, to Harvard University at his own expense, to accept his Prize.

There he said: "I thank you. Two hundred years and finally we have a British winner at a Boston tea party. In honor of this splendid audience, and with the assistance of at least one Nobel Laureate who does not yet know that he is a volunteer, I wish to introduce an extension of my theory. The extension concerns the very difficult and abstruse problem of doughnuts. Doughnuts. Kindly take the doughnut. And now, Professor Glashow, I wish you to demonstrate to this uncomprehending audience my new method of dunking a doughnut."

At which point, Dr. Fisher held up a miniature basketball net, and Nobel Laureate Sheldon Glashow dunked a doughnut through it. Moments later, in a tribute to the accomplishments of tea, doughnuts, and science, a giant artificial doughnut descended on a rope and pulley from the back ceiling of Sanders Theatre, flew over the heads of the audience, and reaching the stage, dunked itself into an attractive, leggy, tap-dancing teacup.

Several days later, Dr. Len Fisher returned to his laboratory, bent on extending his work. He emerged, a year later, with a pair of remarkable discoveries. First, that a biscuit yields more flavor if dunked in a milky drink rather than in plain tea; and, second, that a biscuit dunked in lemonade is not a good thing.

Here is the equation for dunking in hot tea:

$$L^2 = \frac{y \times D \times t}{4 \times \eta}$$

distance that tea penetrates (squared) =
$$\frac{\text{surface tension of tea} \times \text{average pore diameter} \times \text{time in biscuit}}{4 \times \text{viscosity of tea}}$$

EDUCATION

 All sorts of things can teach you a lesson. This chapter describes three great achievements in the field of education:

- Banning the Beaker
- Deepak Chopra
- Dan Quayle

BANNING THE BEAKER

THE OFFICIAL CITATION
THE IG NOBEL CHEMISTRY PRIZE WAS AWARDED TO

Texas State Senator Bob Glasgow, wise writer of logical legislation, for sponsoring the 1989 drug control law that made it illegal to purchase beakers, flasks, test tubes, or other laboratory glassware without a permit.

The glassware regulations are part of the "Texas Controlled Substances Act" as published in article 4476–15 of *Vernon's Texas Civil Statutes* and Sections 17–20 of the Texas Health and Safety Code (481.080) as amended by the 71st Legislature, Regular Session, 1989. For the administrative interpretation of how the law is carried out, see the *Texas Administrative Code*, specifically 37–TAC–13.131.

Some politicians care only about protecting their jobs, but others try very hard to protect the public. A determined few keep watch for things that might be dangerous and can be banned. Texas State Senator Bob Glasgow was extremely determined and extraordinarily watchful.

In 1989, Bob Glasgow persuaded his colleagues in the Texas State Legislature that laboratory glassware—beakers, flasks, and the like—should be considered illegal drug paraphernalia. The legislature agreed. Under Texas law, it is now a Class A misdemeanor to buy, sell, or even give these items without a permit from the state. Those who flout the law are subject to a jail term of up to a year and a fine of up to $4,000.

The Texas Department of Public Safety handles the permit applications. There is an eight-page set of instructions. The permit itself is seven pages long.

Anyone outside Texas should now know that it is illegal to send any of the old laboratory favorites—an Erlenmeyer flask, a Florence flask, a glass funnel, or even the exotically named Soxhlet extractor—to somebody in Texas without first obtaining a permit to do so. The state of Texas will pursue those who recklessly flout Bob Glasgow's restrictions.

Bob Glasgow left the State Senate in 1993. He is now a lawyer in private practice in Stephenville, Texas. His firm's Web site (*www. robertjglasgow.com*) proudly notes that *Texas Monthly* magazine included Glasgow on its "10 Best Legislators" list in 1987. The Web site does not mention that in 1989 the magazine moved Glasgow to its "10 Worst Legislators" list. Bob Glasgow's Web site does, though, mention, without explanation, the curious fact that he served as Governor of Texas on May 11, 1991.

For protecting the public from test tubes and beakers, Bob Glasgow won the 1994 Ig Nobel Prize in the field of Chemistry.

The winner could not, or would not, attend the Ig Nobel Prize Ceremony, and so the Ig Nobel Board of Governors arranged for a major manufacturer of laboratory glassware to give a tribute. Tim Mitchell of Corning, Inc. came to the Ceremony and presented the following thoughts:

"I am here to accept this in lieu of the actual winner. Tonight I'll use this forum to make a few comments on a hot social and scientific issue brought to light by the lawmakers in Texas. That topic is the unregulated and unrestricted sale of test tubes, beakers, and other laboratory apparatus in America.

"There is a grass-roots movement out there to convince the state of Texas to amend their laboratory glassware law. Instead of outlawing glassware altogether, this group would like to see a five-day cooling-off period. They feel this will be enough to discourage people from purchasing a beaker and then using it in a fit of rage to harm themselves or others.

"Part of me wonders, will a waiting period be enough? You see, it only starts with a test tube. You think to yourself, 'Hey, it's only a test tube, for God's sakes.' Pretty soon, though, the rush from a test tube isn't enough. You want to experiment more and more. Then, before you know it, you're laying in the corner of a lab somewhere with a Soxhlet extractor apparatus in one hand, a three-neck flask in the other, strung out and begging for grant money."

DEEPAK CHOPRA

THE OFFICIAL CITATION
THE IG NOBEL PHYSICS PRIZE WAS AWARDED TO

Deepak Chopra of the Chopra Center for Well Being, La Jolla, California, for his unique interpretation of quantum physics as it applies to life, liberty, and the pursuit of economic happiness.

Deepak Chopra has published numerous studies about quantum issues. Two of the best known are *Quantum Healing: Exploring the Frontiers of Mind/Body Medicine,* and *Ageless Body, Timeless Mind: The Quantum Alternative to Growing Old.*

For more than a century, the juiciest mystery in physics has been about quantum mechanics. Specifically: why do the teeny, tiny little quanta of energy and matter seem to behave so weirdly? Physicists assume that if they work hard enough to understand the weirdness, it will turn out to be not weird at all. But one lone, strong voice sings a different tune. To Deepak Chopra, M.D., the weirdness itself is the important thing—and it's something to celebrate, not to understand.

Quantum. The idea started in the year 1900, when Max Karl Ernst Ludwig Planck realized that energy seems to come in extremely tiny amounts—which he called "quanta," all of which are the same size and none of which can be divided into anything smaller. Scientists soon discovered that Planck was correct. He was awarded a Nobel Prize in Physics, and nearly all the Nobel Physics Prizes awarded ever since have, one way or another, been for showing that the weirdness is a little less weird than it at first seemed.

Quantum. Deepak Chopra's Web site *(www.chopra.com)* says that: "He is widely credited with melding modern theories of quantum physics with the timeless wisdom of ancient cultures."

Quantum. In 1989, Deepak Chopra published a book called *Quantum Healing: Exploring the Frontiers of Mind/Body Medicine*. Physicists who see the book typically say that it uses the word "quantum" in ways that would never occur to them. A curious thing about this book called *Quantum Healing* is how seldom the word "quantum" appears in it. Most of those appearances are in the brief chapter called "The Quantum Mechanical Human Body," which contains the following passage:

"The discovery of the quantum realm opened a way to follow the influence of the sun, moon, and sea deeper into ourselves. I am asking you there only in the hope that there is even more healing to be found there. We already know that a human fetus develops by remembering and imitating the shapes of fish, amphibians, and early mammals. Quantum discoveries enable us to go into our very atoms and remember the early universe itself."

Quantum. "The human body first takes form as intense but invisible vibrations, called quantum fluctuations, before it proceeds to coalesce into impulses of energy and particles of matter." (Source: Deepak Chopra)

Quantum. "The most important routine to follow is transcending: the act of getting in touch with the quantum level of yourself." (Source: Deepak Chopra)

Quantum. "Quantum health is based on the idea that we are always, forever, in transition." (Source: Deepak Chopra)

Quantum. The universe consists of a "field of all possibilities" called "the field of pure potentiality," and also the "quantum soup." (Source: Deepak Chopra)

Quantum. At the Chopra Center for Well Being, in La Jolla, California, one can dine at the Quantum Soup Cafe.

Quantum. Inspired by Deepak Chopra, the American Academy of Quantum Medicine, based in Iselin, New Jersey, provides Certification in Quantum Nutrition for health-care providers in the fields of massage therapy, acupuncture, and nutritional counseling, and for certified nutritionists and registered nurses and dieticians, and also for "health-care professionals with a doctorate degree including: MD, OD, DC, DDS, PhD, ND, OMD and IMD."

Quantum. Inspired by Deepak Chopra, a Dr. Stephen Wolinsky developed the fields of Quantum Psychology and Quantum Psychotherapy. Dr. Wolinsky also wrote a book called *Quantum Consciousness*, which is said to bring us full circle in understanding the reality of our inner child.

Quantum. The concept that won Deepak Chopra the 1998 Ig Nobel Prize in the field of Physics.

The winner could not, or would not, attend the Ig Nobel Prize Ceremony. At the ceremony, two distinguished Harvard physics professors paid tribute to him.

Roy Glauber, the Mallinckrodt Professor of Physics, and one of the youngest scientists to have worked on the original atomic bomb project at Los Alamos, said:

"There is not much that I need to tell you about relativistic quantum mechanics. There is not much I *can* tell you about relativistic quantum mechanics. Its achievements in the world of atoms and particles have been great. Its successes, on the other hand, in the world of psychiatry and emotional well-being have been few. And it has certainly not been known for them, particularly. Not, that is, until the recent work of tonight's honoree. Success, of course, is a matter of definition. Relativity and quantum mechanics applied to personal well-being and psychiatry may or may not have done good, but they have certainly done well."

Sheldon Glashow, Higgins Professor of Physics, and winner of a 1979 Nobel Prize in Physics, said:

"I am honored to be here to discuss one of our Laureates. I am one of the few people in this room who have met with him, dined with him, spoken with him. He is held up as a role model to young men and women—high school students throughout the world—at the American Academy of Achievement each year. He is indeed a self-made man.

"Who else could have imagined quantum nutrition? I stand in awe of this man and his accomplishments. I, too, like Professor

Glauber, teach a course called 'Relativistic Quantum Mechanics.' Its lectures are prepared about as well as this lecture is prepared. But I have to say that my course has little more to do with relativistic quantum mechanics than Professor Deepak Chopra's enormous and wonderful opus.

"He is a deserving and wonderful Laureate. Let's hear it for him. DEE-PAK! DEE-PAK! DEE-PAK!"

At this point, the entire crowd joined Professor Glashow in chanting.

THE OFFICIAL CITATION

THE IG NOBEL EDUCATION PRIZE WAS AWARDED TO

J. Danforth Quayle, consumer of time and occupier of space, for demonstrating, better than anyone else, the need for science education.

Dan Quayle was vice president of the US from 1989–1993. During that time, he was also chairman of the National Space Council, and a self-declared champion of education. His was the most inspirational teaching voice of the 20th century. Dan Quayle's words caused people to wonder. He sparked a universal interest in rhetoric and in logic; he made people everywhere appreciate the value of learning.

He leaves a legacy of lessons that are difficult to understand, and even harder to forget. His words sum up the man perhaps better than any description can. Here are some of Dan Quayle's observations.

- What a waste it is to lose one's mind.
- Quite frankly, teachers are the only profession that teach our children.
- We are not ready for any unforeseen event that may or may not occur.
- I have made good judgments in the past. I have made good judgments in the future.
- One word sums up probably the responsibility of any vice president, and that one word is "to be prepared."

- I stand by all the misstatements that I've made.
- My friends, no matter how rough the road may be, we can and we will never, never surrender to what is right.
- [The book *Nicholas, and Alexandra*] was a very good book of Rasputin's involvement in that, which shows how people that are really very weird can get into sensitive positions and have a tremendous impact on history.
- I believe we are on an irreversible trend toward more freedom and democracy, but that could change.
- A low voter turnout is an indication of fewer people going to the polls.
- People are not homeless if they're sleeping in the streets of their own hometowns.
- We [the people of the United States] have a firm commitment to NATO, we are a part of NATO. We have a firm commitment to Europe. We are a part of Europe.
- The global importance of the Middle East is that it keeps the Far East and the Near East from encroaching on each other.
- Bank failures are caused by depositors who don't deposit enough money to cover losses due to mismanagement.
- It isn't pollution that's harming the environment. It's the impurities in our air and water that are doing it.
- [It's] time for the human race to enter the solar system.
- Mars is essentially in the same orbit... Mars is somewhat the same distance from the Sun, which is very important. We have seen pictures where there are canals, we believe, and water. If there is water, that means there is oxygen. If oxygen, that means we can breathe.
- Space is almost infinite. As a matter of fact, we think it is infinite.
- If we do not succeed, then we run the risk of failure.

For so often inspiring people to stop and think, US Vice President J. Danforth Quayle was awarded the 1991 Ig Nobel Prize in the field of Education.

The winner could not, or would not, attend the Ig Nobel Prize Ceremony.

LITERATURE

 Literature is the way many people leave their mark in history. In the following two cases, it is how people earned Ig Nobel Prizes:

- 976 Coauthors in Search of a Title
- The Father of Junk E-mail

976 COAUTHORS IN
SEARCH OF A TITLE

THE OFFICIAL CITATION
THE IG NOBEL LITERATURE PRIZE WAS AWARDED TO

E. Topol, R. Califf, F. Van de Werf, P. W. Armstrong, and their 972 coauthors, for publishing a medical research paper which has one hundred times as many authors as pages.

Their study was published as "An International Randomized Trial Comparing Four Thrombolytic Strategies for Acute Myocardial Infarction," *The New England Journal of Medicine,* **vol. 329, no. 10, September 2, 1993, pp. 673–82.**

In the scientific and medical worlds, having a published paper on the resume can enhance one's prestige. It is not unusual for a paper to have two or more coauthors. It is not unusual to have five or even 10 coauthors. To have 976 coauthors, though, is unusual.

A paper published in 1993 in the *New England Journal of Medicine* has approximately 976 coauthors. The word "approximately" is used here because observers who have tried counting the coauthors disagree as to the exact number, but the total is 976 plus or minus a few. The text of the medical report itself is just a few pages long. All told, the paper has one hundred times as many authors as pages.

The coauthors are in 15 different countries. It is doubtful that all of them have met each other. It is unclear whether even a single one has heard all the names read aloud. Nonetheless, they are coauthors.

For publishing this remarkable paper, the various and sundry coauthors won the 1993 Ig Nobel Prize in the field of Literature.

The winners could not, or would not, attend the Ig Nobel Prize Ceremony, possibly because they could not agree on the wording of an acceptance speech. Had they come, the coauthors would have occupied more than two-thirds of the auditorium where the event was held. Dr. Marcia Angell, the executive editor of the *New England Medical Journal*, accepted the Prize on their behalf. Dr. Angell said:

"On behalf of the *New England Journal of Medicine*, I accept, with dismay, this Prize. I have no idea how many authors we have on that paper. I asked my assistant to count them, and she said she'd rather have a root canal. I estimate there is one author for every two words in this article.

"This is all a part of our continuous author-enhancement campaign. The more papers you have, the more likely you are to be promoted and funded. If everyone can be an author on every paper, then everyone will be a tenured professor, and everyone will have a grant. So who can object to that?"

For a complete list of all 976 coauthors, please visit: www.improbable.com/ig/ig-pastwinners.html

THE FATHER OF
JUNK E-MAIL

THE OFFICIAL CITATION
THE IG NOBEL COMMUNICATIONS PRIZE WAS AWARDED TO

Sanford Wallace, president of Cyber Promotions of Philadelphia—neither rain nor sleet nor dark of night have stayed this self-appointed courier from delivering electronic junk mail to all the world.

Sanford Wallace was called the "King of Spam," "The Most Reviled Man on the Internet," and several thousand other names, all expressing a similar type of admiration. Wallace earned the appellations and the revulsion. Through his efforts, junk E-mail messages became more numerous, in many parts of the earth, than rats, mice, or cockroaches.

Sanford Wallace started a business to help people use the then fairly new medium of electronic mail. Realizing that it was beyond his ability to help everyone, Wallace concentrated on helping people who wanted to send junky advertisements and who were willing to pay an amoral stranger to do it for them.

In the pre-Wallace days on the Internet, there was a widely honored code of good behavior about sending E-mail. The rule of thumb was: don't send unsolicited advertising to strangers.

Because it was so simple and inexpensive to send a message—or a dozen messages, or even several thousand—everyone recognized the potential for annoyance and abuse. Some newcomers to the Internet, unfamiliar with the etiquette, would send out unsolicited ads. Generally they would receive in return an instant flood of complaints, polite and otherwise, and typically they would then temper their behavior.

Sanford Wallace understood the potential for annoyance and abuse. He recognized that in the large numbers of people using E-mail there lay opportunity. If he were to E-mail an ad to ten thousand strangers, one or two might purchase whatever was being advertised. Or maybe one or two people out of a hundred thousand would make a purchase. The fact that 9,999 or 99,999 people might be annoyed was not relevant. And so Sanford Wallace solicited some advertisers and began sending ads on their behalf to thousands upon thousands of strangers.

When the complaints came in, which always happened within minutes of his sending out a new wave of ads, he ignored them. In a surprisingly short amount of time, hundreds of thousands of opportunistic companies were paying Cyber Promotions to send out electronic junk mail for them. And every day millions of people were finding unsolicited junk mail, often in large quantities, flooding into their E-mail accounts.

"If you want to use junk E-mail," Wallace told potential customers, "the bottom line is that it works. It gets results."

Wallace claimed to be sending more than 15 to 20 million pieces of spam a day, and no one doubted his claim. All across the Internet, people came to hate and dread the junk E-mail that poured in on them, dozens or even hundreds of messages day after day, without cease. They loathed spending the time it took to separate their real E-mail messages from the trash that came in with it—the Get Rich Quick schemes, the penis enlargers, the pornographic videotapes, the cut-rate household implements, the fake diplomas from real colleges, and real diplomas from fake universities, and so much more, ever so much more, much too much more.

In no time at all, and for reasons that are not all clear, the word "spam" somehow became the universal term for junk E-mail. The act of sending spam was called "spamming." Sanford Wallace announced that he loved being called "The King of Spam" and would further

enjoy it if people were to call him "Spamford Wallace." The Hormel
Company, manufacturer of the curious foodstuff called Spam (the
consumers of which were honored with an Ig Nobel Prize in 1992,
"for 54 years of undiscriminating digestion"), became enraged at the
hijacking of their product's good, greasy name—and especially at
Sanford Wallace's boastful trumpeting of it—but discovered that
legally they could not put a can on this new use of spam.

Sanford Wallace's business was lucrative and increasingly famous, but it did have problems.

To be able to send E-mail, Cyber Promotions had to have E-mail
accounts. Although several thousand companies were in the business
of providing such accounts, few were willing to have Cyber Promotions as a customer. Whenever he would begin using a new Internet
service provider, it took just hours for outraged spam recipients to
track down the company and inundate it with complaints, threats,
and lawsuits.

This being the Internet, the technical adepts had their own ways
of expressing displeasure. Hackers hacked Cyber Promotion's Web
site, crippling it time and again. These were anonymously altruistic,
if not quite fully law-abiding, programmers who believed it would
be a very public good deed to shut down a very public nuisance.

For a surprisingly long time, Sanford Wallace was unfazed by the
difficulties. They were simply the cost of doing business, and they
were making him a big, albeit detested, name. No matter how many
Internet service providers booted Cyber Promotions off their systems, Wallace always managed to find new ones who would put up
with him for a day or two or three, long enough for him to spew out
several million more E-mails and find yet another Internet service
provider.

For his successful and voluminous efforts to spam the globe,
Sanford Wallace won the 1997 Ig Nobel Prize in the field of Communications.

The winner did not attend the Ig Nobel Prize Ceremony. The Ig
Nobel Board of Governors did not invite him, fearing for the man's
safety.

Over the next few months, Cyber Promotions kept up the good

fight for the right to send annoying, unsolicited E-mail to anyone, anywhere, anytime. Inspired by Wallace's chutzpah, publicity, and client base, competitors multiplied, very much in the manner of cockroaches, mice, and rats.

The incessant lawsuits and the competition together proved too much for the Spam King. In 1998, he abandoned Cyber Promotions. At the same time, he professed to have a change of heart. *Wired News* reported on the spectacle:

"'I will never spam again. Period. I will never be affiliated with spam again. Period.' With those words, Sanford Wallace, the 29-year-old bad boy of the Internet, officially renounced his title as the King of Spam and promised to be good from now on. Not only will he behave, he will announce his support for the Smith Bill—a.k.a. HR 1748, the Netizens Protection Act—federal legislation now before Congress which would outlaw spam . . . As recently as six months ago, Wallace was saying he saw nothing wrong with spam. But now, 'spam has gone too far and the quality of spam has become absolutely disgusting,' he said, adding, 'I take some of the blame for allowing it to go as far as it went.'"

Just days later, a Pennsylvania court found Sanford Wallace guilty of sending unsolicited junk faxes in violation of a 1991 federal law.

The Spam King went on to start up a number of Internet ventures, always claiming to be working against the evils of junk mail, and always somehow providing a substitute of equal power and charm, though of smaller profit margin.

The King's days on the throne may be over, but his influence shines still with the heat of a million bits of glitter. Sanford Wallace opened the door for new generations of spammers, whose clever technical innovations would bring far greater volumes of junk mail, in dazzling variety, to the peoples of the many nations of the earth. He showed them that it could be done, and that probably no one could stop them.

APPENDICES

- Year-by-Year List of Winners
- How to Nominate Someone
- The Web Site
- About the *Annals of Improbable Research*
- Acknowledgments
- Index

Year-by-Year List of Winners

1991

ECONOMICS
Michael Milken, titan of Wall Street and father of the junk bond, to whom the world is indebted.

PEACE
Edward Teller, father of the hydrogen bomb and first champion of the Star Wars weapons system, for his lifelong efforts to change the meaning of peace as we know it.

BIOLOGY
Robert Klark Graham, selector of seeds and prophet of propagation, for his pioneering development of the Repository for Germinal Choice, a sperm bank that accepts donations only from Nobellians and Olympians.

CHEMISTRY
Jacques Benveniste, prolific proseletizer and dedicated correspondent of *Nature*, for his persistent discovery that water, H_2O, is an intelligent liquid, and for demonstrating to his satisfaction that water is able to remember events long after all traces of those events has vanished; and that not only does water have memory, but the information can be transmitted over telephone lines and the Internet.

MEDICINE
Alan Kligerman, deviser of digestive deliverance, vanquisher of vapor, and inventor of Beano, for his pioneering work with anti-

1991 *(continued)*

gas liquids that prevent bloat, gassiness, discomfort, and embarrassment.

EDUCATION
J. Danforth Quayle, consumer of time and occupier of space, for demonstrating, better than anyone else, the need for science education.

LITERATURE
Erich Von Däniken, visionary raconteur and author of *Chariots of the Gods*, for explaining how human civilization was influenced by ancient astronauts from outer space.

1992

ECONOMICS
The investors of Lloyd's of London, heirs to 300 years of dull, prudent management, for their bold attempt to insure disaster by refusing to pay for their company's losses.

PEACE
Daryl Gates, former police chief of the city of Los Angeles, for his uniquely compelling methods of bringing people together.

BIOLOGY
Dr. Cecil Jacobson, relentlessly generous sperm donor, and prolific patriarch of sperm banking, for devising a simple, single-handed method of quality control.

ARCHAEOLOGY
Les Eclaireurs de France, the Protestant youth group whose name means "those who show the way," fresh-scrubbed removers of graffiti, for erasing the ancient paintings from the walls of the Mayrières Cave near the French village of Bruniquel.

1992 *(continued)*

PHYSICS
David Chorley and Doug Bower, lions of low-energy physics, for their circular contributions to field theory based on the geometrical destruction of English crops.

ART
Presented jointly to Jim Knowlton, modern Renaissance man, for his classic anatomy poster "Penises of the Animal Kingdom," and to the US National Endowment for the Arts for encouraging Mr. Knowlton to extend his work in the form of a pop-up book.

MEDICINE
F. Kanda, E. Yagi, M. Fukuda, K. Nakajima, T. Ohta, and O. Nakata of the Shiseido Research Center in Yokohama, for their pioneering research study "Elucidation of Chemical Compounds Responsible for Foot Malodour," especially for their conclusion that people who think they have foot odor do, and those who don't, don't.

CHEMISTRY
Ivette Bassa, constructor of colorful colloids, for her role in the crowning achievement of 20th-century chemistry, the synthesis of bright-blue Jell-O.

NUTRITION
The utilizers of Spam, courageous consumers of canned comestibles, for 54 years of undiscriminating digestion.

LITERATURE
Yuri Struchkov, unstoppable author from the Institute of Organoelemental Compounds in Moscow, for the 948 scientific papers he published between the years 1981 and 1990, averaging more than one every 3.9 days.

1993

ECONOMICS
Ravi Batra of Southern Methodist University, shrewd economist and bestselling author of *The Great Depression of 1990* ($17.95) and *Surviving the Great Depression of 1990* ($18.95), for selling enough copies of his books to single-handedly prevent worldwide economic collapse.

PEACE
The Pepsi-Cola Company of the Philippines, suppliers of sugary hopes and dreams, for sponsoring a contest to create a millionaire, and then announcing the wrong winning number, thereby inciting and uniting 800,000 riotously expectant winners, and bringing many warring factions together for the first time in their nation's history.

MEDICINE
James F. Nolan, Thomas J. Stillwell, and John P. Sands, Jr., medical men of mercy, for their painstaking research report, "Acute Management of the Zipper-Entrapped Penis."

PHYSICS
Louis Kervran of France, ardent admirer of alchemy, for his conclusion that the calcium in chickens' eggshells is created by a process of cold fusion.

CONSUMER ENGINEERING
Ron Popeil, incessant inventor and perpetual pitchman of late-night television, for redefining the industrial revolution with such devices as the Veg-O-Matic, the Pocket Fisherman, Mr. Microphone, and the Inside-the-Shell Egg Scrambler.

VISIONARY TECHNOLOGY
Presented jointly to Jay Schiffman of Farmington Hills, Michigan, crack inventor of AutoVision, an image projection device that makes it possible to drive a car and watch television at the same time, and to the Michigan State Legislature, for making it legal to do so.

1993 (*continued*)

MATHEMATICS

Robert W. Faid of Greenville, South Carolina, farsighted and faithful seer of statistics, for calculating the exact odds (710,609,175,188,282,000 to 1) that Mikhail Gorbachev is the Antichrist.

CHEMISTRY

James Campbell and Gaines Campbell of Lookout Mountain, Tennessee, dedicated deliverers of fragrance, for inventing scent strips, the odious method by which perfume is applied to magazine pages.

BIOLOGY

Paul Williams, Jr., of the Oregon State Health Division, and Kenneth W. Newell of the Liverpool School of Tropical Medicine, bold biological detectives, for their pioneering study, "Salmonella Excretion in Joy-Riding Pigs."

PSYCHOLOGY

John Mack of Harvard Medical School and David Jacobs of Temple University, mental visionaries, for their leaping conclusion that people who believe they were kidnapped by aliens from outer space, probably were—and especially for their conclusion that "the focus of the abduction is the production of children."

LITERATURE

E. Topol, R. Califf, F. Van de Werf, P.W. Armstrong, and their 972 coauthors, for publishing a medical research paper that has one hundred times as many authors as pages.

1994

MEDICINE

This prize is awarded in two parts. First, to Patient X, formerly of the US Marine Corps, valiant victim of a venomous bite from his pet rattlesnake, for his determined use of electroshock therapy: at his

1994 *(continued)*

own insistence, automobile sparkplug wires were attached to his lip, and the car engine revved to 3,000 rpm for five minutes. Second, to Dr. Richard C. Dart of the Rocky Mountain Poison Center and Dr. Richard A. Gustafson of the University of Arizona Health Sciences Center for their well-grounded medical report: "Failure of Electric Shock Treatment for Rattlesnake Envenomation."

PSYCHOLOGY
Lee Kuan Yew, former prime minister of Singapore, practitioner of the psychology of negative reinforcement, for his 30-year study of the effects of punishing four million citizens of Singapore whenever they spat, chewed gum, or fed pigeons.

ECONOMICS
Juan Pablo Davila of Chile, tireless trader of financial futures and former employee of the state-owned Codelco Company, for instructing his computer to "buy" when he meant "sell," and subsequently attempting to recoup his losses by making increasingly unprofitable trades that ultimately lost 0.5% of Chile's gross national product. Davila's relentless achievement inspired his countrymen to coin a new verb: "davilar," meaning, "to botch things up royally."

PEACE
John Hagelin of Maharishi University and the Institute of Science, Technology and Public Policy, promulgator of peaceful thoughts, for his experimental conclusion that 4,000 trained meditators caused an 18% decrease in violent crime in Washington, DC.

ENTOMOLOGY
Robert A. Lopez of Westport, New York, valiant veterinarian and friend of all creatures great and small, for his series of experiments in obtaining ear mites from cats, inserting them into his own ear, and carefully observing and analyzing the results.

1994 (*continued*)

PHYSICS
The Japan Meteorological Agency, for its seven-year study of whether earthquakes are caused by catfish wiggling their tails.

MATHEMATICS
The Southern Baptist Church of Alabama, mathematical measurers of morality, for their county-by-county estimate of how many Alabama citizens will go to hell if they don't repent.

BIOLOGY
W. Brian Sweeney, Brian Krafte-Jacobs, Jeffrey W. Britton, and Wayne Hansen for their breakthrough study, "The Constipated Serviceman: Prevalence Among Deployed US Troops," and especially for their numerical analysis of bowel-movement frequency.

CHEMISTRY
Texas State Senator Bob Glasgow, wise writer of logical legislation, for sponsoring the 1989 drug control law that made it illegal to purchase beakers, flasks, test tubes, or other laboratory glassware without a permit.

LITERATURE
L. Ron Hubbard, ardent author of science fiction and founding father of Scientology, for his crackling Good Book, *Dianetics,* which is highly profitable to mankind or to a portion thereof.

1995

PUBLIC HEALTH
Martha Kold Bakkevig of Sintef Unimed in Trondheim, Norway, and Ruth Nielson of the Technical University of Denmark, for their exhaustive study, "Impact of Wet Underwear on Thermoregulatory Responses and Thermal Comfort in the Cold."

1995 (*continued*)

DENTISTRY
Robert H. Beaumont, of Shoreview, Minnesota, for his incisive study "Patient Preference for Waxed or Unwaxed Dental Floss."

MEDICINE
Marcia E. Buebel, David S. Shannahoff-Khalsa, and Michael R. Boyle, for their invigorating study entitled "The Effects of Unilateral Forced Nostril Breathing on Cognition."

ECONOMICS
Awarded jointly to Nick Leeson and his superiors at Barings Bank, and to Robert Citron of Orange County, California, for using the calculus of derivatives to demonstrate that every financial institution has its limits.

PEACE
The Taiwan National Parliament, for demonstrating that politicians gain more by punching, kicking, and gouging each other than by waging war against other nations.

PSYCHOLOGY
Shigeru Watanabe, Junko Sakamoto, and Masumi Wakita, of Keio University, for their success in training pigeons to discriminate between the paintings of Picasso and those of Monet.

CHEMISTRY
Bijan Pakzad of Beverly Hills, for creating DNA Cologne and DNA Perfume, neither of which contain deoxyribonucleic acid, and both of which come in a triple helix bottle.

PHYSICS
D.M.R. Georget, R. Parker, and A.C. Smith of the Institute of Food Research, Norwich, England, for their rigorous analysis of soggy breakfast cereal, published in the report, "A Study of the Effects of Water Content on the Compaction Behaviour of Breakfast Cereal Flakes."

1995 *(continued)*

NUTRITION

John Martinez of J. Martinez & Company in Atlanta, for Luak Coffee, the world's most expensive coffee, which is made from coffee beans ingested and excreted by the luak (a.k.a., the palm civet), a bobcatlike animal native to Indonesia.

LITERATURE

David B. Busch and James R. Starling, of Madison, Wisconsin, for their deeply penetrating research report, "Rectal Foreign Bodies: Case Reports and a Comprehensive Review of the World's Literature." The citations include reports of, among other items: seven light bulbs; a knife sharpener; two flashlights; a wire spring; a snuff box; an oil can with potato stopper; 11 different forms of fruits, vegetables, and other foodstuffs; a jeweler's saw; a frozen pig's tail; a tin cup; a beer glass; and one patient's remarkable ensemble collection consisting of spectacles, a suitcase key, a tobacco pouch, and a magazine.

1996

PUBLIC HEALTH

Ellen Kleist of Nuuk, Greenland, and Harald Moi of Oslo, Norway, for their cautionary medical report, "Transmission of Gonorrhea Through an Inflatable Doll."

MEDICINE

James Johnston of R.J. Reynolds, Joseph Taddeo of US Tobacco, Andrew Tisch of Lorillard, William Campbell of Philip Morris, Edward A. Horrigan of Liggett Group, Donald S. Johnston of American Tobacco Company, and the late Thomas E. Sandefur, Jr., chairman of Brown and Williamson Tobacco Co., for their unshakable discovery, as testified to the US Congress, that nicotine is not addictive.

1996 (continued)

ECONOMICS
Dr. Robert J. Genco of the University of Buffalo, for his discovery that "financial strain is a risk indicator for destructive periodontal disease."

PEACE
Jacques Chirac, president of France, for commemorating the 50th anniversary of Hiroshima with atomic bomb tests in the Pacific.

BIODIVERSITY
Chonosuke Okamura of the Okamura Fossil Laboratory in Nagoya, Japan, for discovering the fossils of dinosaurs, horses, dragons, princesses, and more than 1,000 other extinct "mini-species," each of which is less than $1/100$ of an inch in length.

PHYSICS
Robert Matthews of Aston University, England, for his studies of Murphy's Law, and especially for demonstrating that toast often falls on the buttered side.

ART
Don Featherstone of Fitchburg, Massachusetts, for his ornamentally evolutionary invention, the plastic pink flamingo.

CHEMISTRY
George Goble of Purdue University, for his blistering world record time for igniting a barbecue grill—three seconds—using charcoal and liquid oxygen.

BIOLOGY
Anders Barheim and Hogne Sandvik of the University of Bergen, Norway, for their tasty and tasteful report, "Effect of Ale, Garlic, and Soured Cream on the Appetite of Leeches."

LITERATURE
The editors of the journal *Social Text*, for eagerly publishing research that they could not understand, that the author said was meaningless, and which claimed that reality does not exist.

1997

PEACE
Harold Hillman of the University of Surrey, England, for his lovingly rendered and ultimately peaceful report, "The Possible Pain Experienced During Execution by Different Methods."

MEDICINE
Carl J. Charnetski and Francis X. Brennan, Jr., of Wilkes University, and James F. Harrison of Muzak Ltd. in Seattle, Washington, for their discovery that listening to elevator Muzak stimulates immunoblobulin A (IgA) production, and thus may help prevent the common cold.

BIOLOGY
T. Yagyu and his colleagues from the University Hospital of Zurich, Switzerland, from Kansai Medical University in Osaka, Japan, and from Neuroscience Technology Research in Prague, Czech Republic, for measuring people's brainwave patterns while they chewed different flavors of gum.

ECONOMICS
Akihiro Yokoi of Wiz Company in Chiba, Japan, and Aki Maita of Bandai Company in Tokyo, the father and mother of Tamagotchi, for diverting millions of person-hours of work into the husbandry of virtual pets.

ENTOMOLOGY
Mark Hostetler of the University of Florida, for his scholarly book, "That Gunk on Your Car," which identifies the insect splats that appear on automobile windows.

ASTRONOMY
Richard Hoagland of New Jersey, for identifying artificial features on the moon and on Mars, including a human face on Mars and ten-mile-high buildings on the far side of the moon.

1997 *(continued)*

PHYSICS
John Bockris of Texas A&M University, for his wide-ranging achievements in cold fusion, in the transmutation of base elements into gold, and in the electrochemical incineration of domestic rubbish.

METEOROLOGY
Bernard Vonnegut of the State University of Albany, for his revealing report, "Chicken Plucking as Measure of Tornado Wind Speed."

LITERATURE
Doron Witztum, Eliyahu Rips, and Yoav Rosenberg of Israel, and Michael Drosnin of the US, for their hairsplitting statistical discovery that the Bible contains a secret, hidden code.

COMMUNICATIONS
Sanford Wallace, president of Cyber Promotions of Philadelphia—neither rain nor sleet nor dark of night have stayed this self-appointed courier from delivering electronic junk mail to all the world.

1998

PEACE
Prime Minister Shri Atal Bihari Vajpayee of India, and Prime Minister Nawaz Sharif of Pakistan, for their aggressively peaceful explosions of atomic bombs.

ECONOMICS
Richard Seed of Chicago, for his efforts to stoke up the world economy by cloning himself and other human beings.

STATISTICS
Jerald Bain of Mt. Sinai Hospital in Toronto, and Kerry Siminoski of the University of Alberta, for their carefully measured report, "The Relationship Among Height, Penile Length, and Foot Size."

1998 (continued)

BIOLOGY
Peter Fong of Gettysburg College, Gettysburg, Pennsylvania, for contributing to the happiness of clams by giving them Prozac.

CHEMISTRY
Jacques Benveniste of France, for his homeopathic discovery that not only does water have memory, but that the information can be transmitted over telephone lines and the Internet.

SAFETY ENGINEERING
Troy Hurtubise, of North Bay, Ontario, for developing and personally testing a suit of armor that is impervious to grizzly bears.

MEDICINE
To Patient Y and to his doctors, Caroline Mills, Meirion Llewelyn, David Kelly, and Peter Holt, of Royal Gwent Hospital, in Newport, Wales, for the cautionary medical report, "A Man Who Pricked His Finger and Smelled Putrid for 5 Years."

SCIENCE EDUCATION
Dolores Krieger, Professor Emerita, New York University, for demonstrating the merits of Therapeutic Touch, a method by which nurses manipulate the energy fields of ailing patients by carefully avoiding physical contact with those patients.

PHYSICS
Deepak Chopra of the Chopra Center for Well Being, La Jolla, California, for his unique interpretation of quantum physics as it applies to life, liberty, and the pursuit of economic happiness.

LITERATURE
Dr. Mara Sidoli of Washington, DC, for her illuminating report, "Farting as a Defence Against Unspeakable Dread."

1999

PEACE
Charl Fourie and Michelle Wong of Johannesburg, South Africa, for inventing an automobile burglar alarm consisting of a detection circuit and a flamethrower.

CHEMISTRY
Takeshi Makino, president of The Safety Detective Agency in Osaka, Japan, for his involvement with S-Check, an infidelity detection spray that wives can apply to their husbands' underwear.

MANAGED HEALTH CARE
The late George and Charlotte Blonsky of New York City and San Jose, California, for inventing a device (US Patent #3,216,423) to aid women in giving birth; the woman is strapped onto a circular table, and the table is then rotated at high speed.

ENVIRONMENTAL PROTECTION
Hyuk-ho Kwon of Kolon Company of Seoul, Korea, for inventing the self-perfuming business suit.

BIOLOGY
Dr. Paul Bosland, director of the Chile Pepper Institute, New Mexico State University, Las Cruces, New Mexico, for breeding a spiceless jalapeño chile pepper.

LITERATURE
The British Standards Institution, for its six-page specification (BS 6008) of the proper way to make a cup of tea.

SOCIOLOGY
Steve Penfold of York University in Toronto, for doing his Ph.D. thesis on the sociology of Canadian donut shops.

PHYSICS
Dr. Len Fisher of Bath, England, and Sydney, Australia, for calculating the optimal way to dunk a biscuit

... and ...

1999 (*continued*)

Professor Jean-Marc Vanden-Broeck of the University of East Anglia, England, and Belgium, for calculating how to make a teapot spout that does not drip.

MEDICINE
Dr. Arvid Vatle of Stord, Norway, for carefully collecting, classifying, and contemplating which kinds of containers his patients chose when submitting urine samples.

SCIENCE EDUCATION
The Kansas State Board of Education and the Colorado State Board of Education, for mandating that children should not believe in Darwin's theory of evolution any more than they believe in Newton's theory of gravitation, Faraday's and Maxwell's theory of electromagnetism, or Pasteur's theory that germs cause disease.

2000

PSYCHOLOGY
David Dunning of Cornell University, and Justin Kruger of the University of Illinois, for their modest report, "Unskilled and Unaware of It: How Difficulties in Recognizing One's Own Incompetence Lead to Inflated Self-Assessments."

PEACE
The British Royal Navy, for ordering its sailors to stop using live cannon shells, and instead just to shout "Bang!"

CHEMISTRY
Donatella Marazziti, Alessandra Rossi, and Giovanni B. Cassano of the University of Pisa, and Hagop S. Akiskal of the University of California (San Diego), for their discovery that, biochemically, romantic love may be indistinguishable from having severe obsessive-compulsive disorder.

2000 (*continued*)

ECONOMICS
The Reverend Sun Myung Moon, for bringing efficiency and steady growth to the mass-marriage industry, with, according to his reports, a 36-couple wedding in 1960, a 430-couple wedding in 1968, an 1,800-couple wedding in 1975, a 6,000-couple wedding in 1982, a 30,000-couple wedding in 1992, a 360,000-couple wedding in 1995, and a 36,000,000-couple wedding in 1997.

MEDICINE
Willibrord Weijmar Schultz, Pek van Andel, and Eduard Mooyaart of Groningen, the Netherlands, and Ida Sabelis of Amsterdam, for their illuminating report, "Magnetic Resonance Imaging of Male and Female Genitals During Coitus and Female Sexual Arousal."

PUBLIC HEALTH
Jonathan Wyatt, Gordon McNaughton, and William Tullet of Glasgow, for their alarming report, "The Collapse of Toilets in Glasgow."

PHYSICS
Andre Geim of the University of Nijmegen, the Netherlands, and Sir Michael Berry of Bristol University, England, for using magnets to levitate a frog.

COMPUTER SCIENCE
Chris Niswander of Tucson, Arizona, for inventing PawSense, software that detects when a cat is walking across your computer keyboard.

BIOLOGY
Richard Wassersug of Dalhousie University, for his first-hand report, "On the Comparative Palatability of Some Dry-Season Tadpoles from Costa Rica."

LITERATURE
Jasmuheen (formerly known as Ellen Greve) of Australia, first lady of Breatharianism, for her book *Living on Light,* which explains that although some people do eat food, they don't ever really need to.

2001

PUBLIC HEALTH
Chittaranjan Andrade and B.S. Srihari of the National Institute of
Mental Health and Neurosciences, Bangalore, India, for their probing
medical discovery that nose picking is a common activity among adolescents.

PSYCHOLOGY
Lawrence W. Sherman of Miami University, Ohio, for his influential
research report, "An Ecological Study of Glee in Small Groups of
Preschool Children."

ECONOMICS
Joel Slemrod of the University of Michigan Business School, and
Wojciech Kopczuk of the University of British Columbia, for their
conclusion that people find a way to postpone their deaths if that
would qualify them for a lower rate on the inheritance tax.

PEACE
Viliumas Malinauskas of Grutas, Lithuania, for creating the amusement park known as "Stalin World."

MEDICINE
Peter Barss of McGill University, for his impactful medical report,
"Injuries Due to Falling Coconuts."

PHYSICS
David Schmidt of the University of Massachusetts, for his partial solution to the question of why shower curtains billow inward.

TECHNOLOGY
Awarded jointly to John Keogh of Hawthorn, Victoria, Australia, for
patenting the wheel in the year 2001, and to the Australian Patent
Office, for granting him Innovation Patent #2001100012.

ASTROPHYSICS
Dr. Jack and Rexella Van Impe of Jack Van Impe Ministries, Rochester
Hills, Michigan, for their discovery that black holes fulfill all the tech-
nical requirements to be the location of hell.

2001 (*continued*)

BIOLOGY
Buck Weimer of Pueblo, Colorado, for inventing Under-Ease, airtight underwear with a replaceable charcoal filter that removes bad-smelling gases before they escape.

LITERATURE
John Richards of Boston, England, founder of the Apostrophe Protection Society, for his efforts to protect, promote, and defend the differences between plural and possessive.

2002

BIOLOGY
Norma E. Bubier, Charles G.M. Paxton, Phil Bowers, and D. Charles Deeming of the UK, for their report "Courtship Behaviour of Ostriches Towards Humans Under Farming Conditions in Britain."

PHYSICS
Arnd Leike of the University of Munich, for demonstrating that beer froth obeys the mathematical Law of Exponential Decay.

INTERDISCIPLINARY RESEARCH
Karl Kruszelnicki of the University of Sydney, for performing a comprehensive survey of human belly button lint—who gets it, when, what color, and how much.

CHEMISTRY
Theodore Gray of Wolfram Research, in Champaign, Illinois, for gathering many elements of the periodic table, and assembling them into the form of a four-legged periodic table table.

MATHEMATICS
K.P. Sreekumar and the late G. Nirmalan of Kerala Agricultural University, India, for their analytical report, "Estimation of the Total Surface Area in Indian Elephants."

2002 (*continued*)

LITERATURE
Vicki L. Silvers of the University of Nevada-Reno, and David S. Kreiner of Central Missouri State University, for their colorful report, "The Effects of Pre-Existing Inappropriate Highlighting on Reading Comprehension."

PEACE
Keita Sato, president of Takara Co., Dr. Matsumi Suzuki, president of Japan Acoustic Lab, and Dr. Norio Kogure, executive director, Kogure Veterinary Hospital, for promoting peace and harmony between the species by inventing Bow-Lingual, a computer-based automatic dog-to-human language translation device.

HYGIENE
Eduardo Segura of Lavakan de Aste, in Tarragona, Spain, for inventing a washing machine for cats and dogs.

ECONOMICS
The executives, corporate directors, and auditors of Enron, Lernout & Hauspie [Belgium], Adelphia, Bank of Commerce and Credit International [Pakistan], Cendant, CMS Energy, Duke Energy, Dynegy, Gazprom [Russia], Global Crossing, HIH Insurance [Australia], Informix, Kmart, Maxwell Communications [UK], McKessonHBOC, Merrill Lynch, Merck, Peregrine Systems, Qwest Communications, Reliant Resources, Rent-Way, Rite Aid, Sunbeam, Tyco, Waste Management, WorldCom, Xerox, and Arthur Andersen, for adapting the mathematical concept of imaginary numbers for use in the business world. [Note: all companies are US-based unless otherwise noted.]

MEDICINE
Chris McManus of University College, London, for his excruciatingly balanced report, "Scrotal Asymmetry in Man and in Ancient Sculpture."

How to Nominate Someone

OFFICIAL CRITERION FOR WINNING A PRIZE: Ig Nobel Prizes are given for "achievements that cannot or should not be reproduced."

UNOFFICIAL CRITERION FOR WINNING A PRIZE: A winning achievement must first make people *laugh*, then make them *think*.

WHO IS AUTHORIZED TO SEND IN NOMINATIONS: Anyone.

WHO IS ELIGIBLE TO WIN: Anyone, anywhere. All sorts of people get unusual ideas, and vow to act on them. Those destined to win an Ig Nobel Prize get very unusual ideas, and don't bother to make vows—they simply swing into action. Shoes and ships; cabbages and kings; centrifugal birthing machines and leech appetite stimulants; the drafting of comprehensive technical specifications for making a cup of tea; the classification of foreign objects found in the rectums of medical patients—any of these could be the basis for an Ig Nobel Prize-winning achievement. And most of them have been. You can nominate a stranger, a colleague, a boss, a spouse, or yourself. You can nominate an individual or a group.

WHO IS NOT ELIGIBLE TO WIN: People who are fictional or whose existence—and achievement—cannot be verified.

CATEGORIES: Once the winners are selected, each Prize is given in a particular category. Some categories recur every year—Biology, Medicine, Physics, Peace, Economics. Other categories (Safety Engineering, Environmental Protection) are created to fit the particular and/or peculiar nature of a particular achievement. But, in truth, it is impossible to confine Ig Nobel Prize winners within categories. (It is not, however, impossible to confine Ig Nobel Prize winners. Many winners of the Economics Prize, for example, have been unable to attend the Ig Nobel Prize Ceremony because they were serving a prior engagement of five to fifteen years.)

GOODNESS OR BADNESS: Every year, of the 10 new Ig Nobel Prizes, about half are awarded for things that most people would say are commendable—if perhaps goofy. The other half go for things that are, in some people's eyes, less commendable. All judgments as to "goodness" and/or "badness" are entirely up to each observer.

HOW TO SEND IN A NOMINATION: Gather information that explains *who* the nominee is and *what* the nominee has accomplished. Please include enough information that the judges can get an immediate, clear appreciation of why a candidate deserves an Ig Nobel Prize. Also indicate where the judges can find further information if they need it, including (if you know it) how we can get in touch with the nominee. Mail or E-mail the nomination to:

> Ig Nobel Nominations
> c/o Annals of Improbable Research
> P.O. Box 380853
> Cambridge, MA 02238 USA
>
> air@improbable.com

If you mail the material and would like a response, please include an E-mail address or an adequately stamped, self-addressed envelope. If you wish anonymity, you can have it. The Ig Nobel Board of Governors typically loses or discards most of its records, in any event.

You can find further information at the *Annals of Improbable Research* Web site (*www.improbable.com*).

The Web Site

The Ig Nobel Prizes' home page is at *www.improbable.com.*

It is part of the *Annals of Improbable Research* Web site.

There you will find a complete list of the winners and, in many cases, links to their home pages, their original research, and press clippings about them. You will also find video from some of the ceremonies, and links to the recordings of the annual Ig Nobel broadcast on National Public Radio's *Talk of the Nation/Science Friday with Ira Flatow* program. We also put up occasional news of the continuing adventures of past Ig Nobel Prize winners.

Free Newsletter: To keep informed of upcoming Ig Nobel ceremonies and related events, add yourself to the distribution list for the free monthly newsletter mini-AIR. You can do that at the Web site or, alternatively:

Send a brief E-mail message to this address:

LISTPROC@AIR.HARVARD.EDU

The body of your message should contain *only* the words "SUBSCRIBE MINI-AIR" followed by your name. Here are two examples:

SUBSCRIBE MINI-AIR Irene Curie Joliot
SUBSCRIBE MINI-AIR Nicholai Lobachevsky

About the Annals of Improbable Research

The *Annals of Improbable Research* (*AIR*) is a humor magazine about science, medicine, and technology. It may be the only science journal read not just by scientists and doctors, but also by their family and friends.

AIR is known for:

- funny, genuine research, culled from somber science and medical journals;
- deadpan satire; and
- the Ig Nobel Prizes.

About a third of what we publish in *AIR* is genuine research, about a third is concocted, and about a third of our readers cannot tell the difference. (In the magazine, we always indicate which items come from official sources—and we even give you the info to go look and see for yourself.)

Every year, we devote one issue to a full report on the Ig Nobel Prize Ceremony, with all the juicy details, lots of photos, and all the words for that year's Ig Nobel mini-opera. You can subscribe to the magazine (6 issues per year) by going to the Web site (*www.improbable.com*), or by mail or telephone:

Mail: Annals of Improbable Research
P.O. Box 380853
Cambridge, MA 02238 USA

Telephone: (617) 491-4437
Fax: (617) 661-0927
E-mail: air@improbable.com

See page 241 for a handy subscription form.

Acknowledgments

This book is for Robin.

Special Ig thanks to Sid Abrahams, Margot Button, Sip Siperstein, Don Kater, Stanley Eigen, Jackie Baum, Joe Wrinn, Gary Dryfoos, the Harvard Computer Society, the Harvard-Radcliffe Science Fiction Society, and the Harvard-Radcliffe Society of Physics Students.

Special publishing thanks to Regula Noetzli, Trevor Dolby, Pandora White, Alexa Dalby, Mitch Hoffman, and Stephanie Bowe.

Every year, between 50 and 100 people help organize the Ig Nobel Prize Ceremony. The ceremony and this book would not have been possible without a very lot of help from a very large number of people. Among them:

Danny Adams, Alan Asadorian and Dorian Photo Lab, Brad Barnhorst, Referee John Barrett, Steve Beeber, Margaret Ann Brady, Charles Bergquist, Doug Berman, Silvery Jim Bredt, Blinsky, Alan Brody, Jeff Bryant, Nick Carstoiu, Jon Chase, Keith Clark, Jon Connor, Sylvie Coyaud, Frank Cunningham, Cybercom.net, Investigator T. Divens, Bob Dushman, Dorothy Dwyer, Kate Eppers, Relena Erskine, Dave Feldman, Len Finegold, Ira Flatow, Stefanie Friedhoff, Jerry Friedman, Greg Garrison, and the library staff at the *Birmingham News*, Bruce Gellerman, Sheila Gibson, Shelly Glashow, Margaret Ann Gray, Deborah Henson-Conant, Jeff Hermes, Dudley Herschbach, Holly Hodder, David Holzman, Karen Hopkin, Jo Rita Jordan, Roger Kautz, Hoppin' Harpaul Kohli, Alex Kohn, Deb Kreuze, Leslie Lawrence, Matt Lena, Jerry and Maggie Lettvin, Barbara Lewis, Tom Lehrer, Harry Lipkin, Colonel Bill Lipscomb, Alan Litsky, Julia

Lunetta, Counter-Clockwise Mahoney, Lois Malone, Prominent New York attorney William J. Maloney, Mary Chung Restaurant, Micheline Mathews-Roth, Les Frères Michel, the MIT Museum, MIT Press Bookstore, David Molnar, Carol Morton, Lisa Mullins, the Museum of Bad Art, Steve Nadis, Mary O'Grady, Bob Park, Jay Pasachoff, the Flying Petscheks, Stephen Powell, Harriet Provine, Sophie Renaud, Boyce Rensberger, Genevieve Reynolds, Rich Roberts, Nailah Robinson, Nicki Rohloff, Bob Rose, Daniel, Isabelle, Katrina, Natasha, and Sylvia Rosenberg, Louise Sacco, Rob Sanders, the entire magnificent gang at Sanders Theatre, Margo Seltzer, Roland Sharrillo, Sally Shelton, Miles Smith, Smitty Smith, Kris Snibbe, Earle Spamer, Chris Small, Naomi Stephen, Alan Symonds, Judy Taylor, Chris Thorpe, Peaco Todd, Clockwise Twersky, Tom and Brenda Ulrich, Ami Vora, Mark Waldstein, Verena Wieloch, Bob Wilson, Eric Workman, Howard Zaharoff, and, finally, an infinity of thanks to Martin Gardner.

And, of course, thank you—on behalf of all of us—to the Ig Nobel Prize winners, and to everyone who has sent in nominations. As we say at the end of each year's ceremony: "If you didn't win an Ig Nobel Prize—and especially if you did—better luck next year!"

INDEX

ABOUT THE *ANNALS OF IMPROBABLE RESEARCH*

The *Annals of Improbable Research (AIR)* is a humor magazine about science, medicine, and technology. It may be the only science journal read not just by scientists and doctors, but also by their family and friends.

AIR is known for:
- funny, genuine research, culled from somber science and medical journals;
- deadpan satire; and
- the Ig Nobel Prizes.

About a third of what we publish in *AIR* is genuine research, about a third is concocted, and about a third of our readers cannot tell the difference. (In the magazine we always indicate which items come from official sources—and we even give you the info to go look and see for yourself.)

Every year, we devote one issue to a full report on the Ig Nobel Prize Ceremony, with all the juicy details, lots of photos, and all the words for that year's Ig Nobel mini-opera. You can subscribe to the magazine (6 issues per year) by going to the Web site (www.improbable.com), or by mail or telephone:

HERE IS A HANDY SUBSCRIPTION FORM

PLEASE ☐ START OR ☐ RENEW A SUBSCRIPTION FOR ME ☐ 1 YEAR (6 ISSUES) ☐ 2 YEARS (12 ISSUES)
☐ START OR ☐ RENEW A GIFT SUBSCRIPTION ☐ 1 YEAR (6 ISSUES) ☐ 2 YEARS (12 ISSUES)

MY NAME, ADDRESS AND ALL THAT

NAME . . . .

ADDRESS . . . .

. . . .

. . . .

. . . .

. . . .

. . . .

PHONE . . . .

FAX . . . .

E-MAIL . . . .

I AM GIVING A SUBSCRIPTION TO

NAME . . . .

ADDRESS . . . .

. . . .

. . . .

. . . .

. . . .

. . . .

. . . .

FAX . . . .

E-MAIL . . . .

☐ SEND RENEWAL NOTICE TO MY BENEFICIARY

☐ SEND RENEWAL NOTICE TO ME

RATES (IN US DOLLARS)

USA	$29	$53
CANADA/MEX	$33	$57
OVERSEAS	$45	$82

TOTAL PAYMENT ENCLOSED . . . .

PAYMENT METHOD

☐ CHECK (DRAWN ON US BANK) OR INTERNATIONAL MONEY ORDER

☐ MASTERCARD ☐ VISA ☐ DISCOVER

CARD NUMBER . . . . EXP. DATE . . . .

Send payment to: Annals of Improbable Research
PO Box 380853
Cambridge
MA 02238
USA

Telephone: (617) 491-4437
Fax: (617) 661-0927
E-mail: air@improbable.com

www.improbable.com